FINANCE FOR SMALL BUSINESSES

BUSINESS GUIDEBOOKS

SELF-HELP GUIDES FOR SMALL BUSINESSMEN

FINANCE FOR SMALL BUSINESSES

KEITH CHECKLEY
FELLOW OF THE INSTITUTE OF BANKERS

SERIES FOREWORD BY DAVID TRIPPIER,
UNDER SECRETARY OF STATE AT THE
DEPARTMENT OF INDUSTRY

Sphere Study Aids

Sphere Study Aids
30/32 Gray's Inn Road
London
WC1X 8JL

First published by
Sphere Books Ltd 1984

Typeset by H.M. Repros, Glasgow.
Printed and bound in Great Britain by
Cox & Wyman Ltd, Reading

CONTENTS

SERIES FOREWORD

by David Trippier MP,
Parliamentary Under Secretary of State for Industry

The environment for small businesses has changed greatly for the better in the past four years. An effective Loan Guarantee Scheme and generous tax relief through the Business Expansion Scheme are only two of many in over 100 Government measures to provide incentives and remove obstacles to business enterprise. Our efforts are complemented by a welcome improvement in attitudes in commerce and industry towards the small business operator.

Vital though these changes are, the success of any new expanding business will always depend on the skill, knowledge and tenacity of those running the firm. Practical sources of expertise and advice, as provided by this series of business Guidebooks, are invaluable aids for the busy entrepreneur. General business management and finance, without doubt, cause the most problems and biggest headaches for the small firm.

Certainly many young businesses have been given a better chance of success by the increasing availability of help with the particular challenges that beset them. I am encouraged by figures which show for the two years, 1981 and 1982, 'births' of new firms well in excess of 'deaths' in spite of the worldwide economic recession.

A flourishing small firms sector in any national economy brings new energy, new enterprise and new initiatives into industry and commerce. These attributes have never been more necessary than in today's tough economic climate and highly competitive world markets. To this end, these business Guidebooks will be a worthwhile investment for every new and expanding business.

INTRODUCTION

Small businesses are undoubtedly an important part of our economy. Furthermore, they employ a large percentage of our working population.

I firmly believe that an essential ingredient for success is an understanding of finance. Not only how to obtain it but how to use it effectively in the development of your particular business.

In this book I discuss the merits of financial planning, explaining simple techniques to help you monitor the health of your business. Also how to present your case for finance and where to get it! Also included are details of the 88 Government schemes that are currently available. Finally, there is a chapter on key areas for business control.

I sincerely hope you enjoy reading the book and that it proves of use to you in the development of your business.

I am grateful to the following organisations for their help in providing statistics and information:

The Investors Chronicle
The Government Statistics and Market Intelligence Library.
The Industrial and Commercial Finance Corporation.
Yorkshire and Humberside Development Association.
The Bank of England Industrial Finance Division.
The Department of Industry
Bank Information Services
The House of Commons Research Library
The European Commission

and to the following individuals: John Spence M.P.; Keith Dickinson; to my sister Sheila for her patient typing and to my researcher Miss Elaine Ball.

Keith Checkley
Bilbrough,
York.
September, 1983

1. The General Scene

A definition

The first major study of small businesses was published in 1971. This *Report of the Committee of Inquiry on Small Firms* was chaired by J. E. Bolton. Many significant points were made in the report as to the structure and financial needs of small businesses.
The *Bolton Report* (as it is commonly known) found that defining a small business was difficult in that employment of assets, turnover, output, employees or whatever measure used may not be applicable to each and every sector of small businesses.
However an adoption had to be made for each sector and was as follows.

Table 1
Small firm sector as defined by the Bolton Committee

Industry	*Statistical definition of small firms used by the Committee*	*Small firms (as defined) as a % of all firms in the industry 1963* %	*Average employment per small firm 1963*
Manufacturing	200 employees or less	94	25
Retailing	turnover £50,000 pa or less (1963 prices)	96	3
Wholesale trades	turnover £200,000 pa or less (1963 prices)	77	7
Construction	25 employees or less	89	6
Mining/ quarrying	25 employees or less	77	11
Motor trades	turnover £100,000 pa or less (1963 prices)	87	3
Miscellaneous services	turnover £50,000 pa or less (1963 prices)	90	4
Road transport	5 vehicles or less	85	4
Catering	All except multiples & brewery managed public houses	96	3

Table 2
Analysis of business by turnover size

Trade classification	Turnover band (£'000) 0–16	17–49	50–99	100–249	250–499	500–999
Agriculture	56 718 (35)	55 337 (34)	27 742 (17)	17 696 (11)	4 287 (3)	1 530 (1)
Mining and quarrying and public utilities	419 (23)	220 (12)	207 (12)	301 (17)	171 (10)	137 (8)
Manufacturing industries	24 887 (17)	34 619 (23)	23 336 (16)	27 066 (18)	14 166 (9)	10 060 (7)
Food, drink and tobacco	1 059 (11)	1 813 (19)	1 733 (18)	1 828 (19)	923 (10)	615 (6)
Coal and petroleum products	28 (12)	28 (12)	26 (11)	39 (16)	21 (9)	24 (10)
Chemicals and allied industries	613 (15)	607 (15)	454 (11)	673 (16)	447 (11)	403 (10)
Metal manufacture	306 (10)	508 (17)	368 (12)	533 (18)	332 (11)	290 (10)
Mechanical engineering	4 262 (17)	5 909 (23)	3 943 (15)	4 780 (19)	2 524 (10)	1 731 (7)
Instrument engineering	637 (20)	685 (22)	452 (15)	528 (17)	272 (9)	224 (7)
Electrical engineering	2 027 (20)	2 265 (22)	1 395 (14)	1 671 (16)	905 (9)	650 (6)
Shipbuilding and marine engineering	522 (23)	540 (24)	326 (14)	366 (16)	187 (8)	119 (5)
Vehicles	209 (13)	231 (15)	160 (10)	221 (14)	167 (11)	165 (11)
Metal goods not elsewhere specified	2 811 (16)	4 129 (23)	2 743 (16)	3 454 (20)	1 778 (10)	1 148 (7)
Textiles	880 (13)	1 179 (18)	885 (14)	1 116 (17)	703 (11)	662 (10)
Leather, leather goods and fur	314 (15)	523 (26)	338 (17)	378 (19)	198 (10)	106 (5)
Clothing and footwear	1 374 (12)	2 828 (25)	2 346 (21)	2 257 (20)	888 (8)	636 (6)
Bricks, pottery, glass, cement etc	513 (17)	639 (21)	393 (13)	434 (15)	290 (10)	223 (7)
Timber, furniture etc	2 539 (19)	3 690 (28)	1 909 (14)	2 133 (16)	1 149 (9)	790 (6)
Paper, printing and publishing	4 132 (18)	5 738 (26)	3 626 (16)	4 025 (18)	1 984 (9)	1 261 (6)
Other manufacturing industries	2 661 (18)	3 307 (23)	2 239 (15)	2 630 (18)	1 398 (10)	1 013 (7)
Construction	58 067 (29)	75 204 (37)	27 871 (14)	22 532 (11)	8 935 (4)	4 866 (2)
Road transport and transport services	13 287 (22)	22 991 (39)	7 601 (13)	7 288 (12)	3 574 (6)	2 201 (4)
Wholesaling and dealing	16 039 (15)	22 783 (21)	17 234 (16)	21 171 (19)	11 914 (11)	9 006 (8)
Retailing	26 714 (10)	100 376 (38)	74 048 (28)	48 231 (18)	10 583 (4)	3 860 (1)
Finance, property and professional services	32 256 (34)	30 165 (32)	11 520 (12)	11 091 (12)	4 319 (5)	2 479 (3)
Catering	9 684 (8)	51 876 (44)	36 192 (30)	16 932 (14)	2 903 (2)	846 (1)
Motor trades	11 135 (15)	21 535 (29)	11 317 (15)	13 008 (18)	7 076 (10)	4 930 (7)
Other services	46 323 (30)	60 482 (39)	20 111 (13)	15 575 (10)	5 631 (4)	3 235 (2)
Total	**295 529 (21)**	**475 588 (34)**	**257 179 (18)**	**200 891 (14)**	**73 559 (5)**	**43 150 (3)**

1000–4999	5000 and over	Total
621 (—)	86 (—)	164 017
195 (11)	139 (8)	1 789
11 761 (8)	4 557 (3)	150 452
990 (10)	695 (7)	9 656
41 (17)	35 (14)	242
593 (14)	395 (9)	4 185
435 (14)	259 (9)	3 031
1 890 (7)	663 (3)	25 702
257 (8)	61 (2)	3 116
829 (8)	415 (4)	10 157
156 (7)	62 (3)	2 278
238 (15)	158 (10)	1 549
1 203 (7)	315 (2)	17 581
840 (13)	285 (4)	6 550
156 (8)	23 (1)	2 036
663 (6)	153 (1)	11 145
345 (12)	152 (5)	2 989
841 (6)	185 (1)	13 236
1 228 (5)	407 (2)	22 401
1 056 (7)	294 (2)	14 598
3 730 (2)	894 (—)	202 099
1 903 (3)	416 (1)	59 261
9 879 (9)	2 477 (2)	110 503
2 167 (1)	626 (—)	266 605
2 370 (2)	1 392 (1)	95 592
478 (—)	107 (—)	119 018
4 189 (6)	740 (1)	73 930
3 198 (2)	1 363 (1)	155 918
40 491 (3)	**12 797 (1)**	**1 399 184**

It is most revealing to note that on this information (Table 2) derived from the Business Statistics Office — more than 90% of businesses have a turnover of less than £1M. (Figures in brackets.) The total number of firms 'registered' is 1 399 194. Comparing this 1982 chart with the 1980 statistics shows a 5% increase.

It is worth mentioning the high percentage figures revealed but the low number of average employees. In formulating these sector definitions the Committee of Inquiry had the following business characteristics in mind: (i) In economic terms, a small firm is one that has a relatively small share of its market, (ii) an essential characteristic of a small firm is that it is managed by its owners in a personalised way. (iii) It is independent in the sense that it does not form part of a larger enterprise which can provide a financial umbrella; (iv) the owner-managers should be free from outside control in taking their principal decisions.
The turnover bands shown in Table 1 are now of course way out of date due to inflationary trends. Perhaps a broad definition of a small business would be acceptable as 'a small business is one employing less than 200 people; and having an annual turnover of less than £3 million.'

Table 3 Comparison between 1980 and 1982 counts

Trade classification	Number of legal units 1980 (000)	Number of legal units 1982 (000)	Percentage change (1980–1982)
Agriculture	162	164	+ 1
Production	143	152	+ 6
Construction	193	202	+ 5
Road transport and transport services	58	59	+ 2
Wholesaling and dealing	100	111	+11
Retailing	265	267	+ 1
Finance, property and professional services	88	96	+ 9
Catering	116	119	+ 3
Motor trades	71	74	+ 4
Other services	136	156	+15
Total	1 332	1 399	+ 5

The importance of the small business sector

The *Bolton Report* indicated the principal functions of the sector as:

1. Providing outlets for large numbers of individualistic people who preferred to work in small units.
2. Providing an essential source of suppliers to large firms.
3. Performing a highly economic role in those areas where a large variety of products and where customer service was of key importance.
4. Providing variety of choice for the consumer.
5. Contributing towards a balanced and stable industrial structure.
6. Offering an essential source of innovation, and a seed-bed for large firms of the future.
7. Furnishing a source of entirely new industries.
8. Maintaining a means of entry to business for new entrepreneurial talent.

The importance of the small business within our economy has already been briefly indicated in Table 1. We can reinforce our opinions by looking at further statistics shown in Table 2.

The total businesses registered has gone up from 1 331 681 to 1 399 194 (+5%). As regards sector analysis — the smallest growth has been in the agriculture and retailing sections (+ 1%).
If we now look for where the overall business growth has occurred again, it is at the lower end of the turnover range with an increase of 60 089 businesses. See Table 4.

Table 4
Businesses with:

	Turnover less than £1m	More than £1m	Totals	
1982	1345896	53238	1399184	No. of units
1980	1285807	45874	1331681	No. of units
difference	+ 60089	+ 7414	+ 67503	

Looking back at Table 2 the most units registered are in the retailing; construction; agriculture and manufacturing sectors.

Retailing	266605
Construction	202099
Agriculture	164017
Manufacturing	150452

Census of employment

Again there is a predominance of employees at the small business end.

Table 5
Census of Employment Units: size analysis 1976

1976 Great Britain

Size bands according to numbers of employees	Numbers of census units	Numbers of employees
1	162 352	162 352
2	146,038	292 076
3–4	196,440	675 600
5–10	246 110	1 698 848
11–24	149 683	2 372 872
25–49	66 954	2 288 165
50–99	33 881	2 338 690
100–199	18 340	2 536 082
200–499	10 649	3 227 142
500–999	3 098	2 122 805
1 000–1 999	1 335	1 820 273
2 000–4 999	474	1 368 540
5 000 +	94	762 646
Total	1 035 448	21 666 091*

Analysing this table bearing in mind our definition of less than 200 employees; it shows that over 90% of the census units were small businesses and furthermore that they employed over 50% of the total number of employees in employment.

Census of production

If we take as an example all manufacturing industries, the total employees is 7.5m over 86 954 establishments. See Table 6.

Table 6

All manufacturing industries	Size Group	Establishments Number	Employment Total Thousands
	1–10	37 878	195.4
	-24	22 261	378.2
	25–99	15 122	797.3
	100–199	5 027	691.3
	200–499	4 050	1 269.8
	500–999	1 459	1 021.3
	1 000–1 499	490	605.0
	1 500 & over	667	2 563.6
	Total	86 954	7 521.9

Again, it is significant at the less than 200 employees band. Also if we analyse the output from these groupings it represents 24% of total output. See Table 7.

Table 7

Size Groups	Total Sales and Work done £ million
1–10	8 304.9
11–24	
25–99	
100–199	4 558.0
200–499	9 103.1
500–999	7 180.3
1 000–1 499	4 400.7
1 500 and over	19 763.1
Total	53 309.9

Births and deaths of firms in the U.K.

The Department of Industry have produced provisional figures to show the trends over 1980–1982.

Table 8
Provisional estimates for 1980-82: Births and deaths of firms by sector in the UK

Year	Trend	Agriculture	Production	Construction	Transport
1980	Births	5 200	10 300	17 500	4 800
revised	Deaths	5 200	10 200	14 900	5 900
	Surplus	—	100	2 600	1 100
1981	Births	5 500	12 300	18 200	5 200
provisional	Deaths	4 500	10 100	12 800	5 300
	Surplus	1 000	2 100	5 400	– 100
1982	Births	2 900	13 700	17 800	5 900
provisional	Deaths	4 500	11 100	14 400	5 200
	Surplus	– 1 600	2 600	3 400	700
1980–1982	Births	13 600	36 300	53 500	15 900
provisional	Deaths	14 200	31 400	42 100	16 400
	Surplus	– 600	4 800	11 400	– 500

This table illustrates more births than deaths in 1981 and 1982 (+14800 and +7000) as compared with a deficit of 2000 in 1980.

Overall, 1980–82 there were	363 100 births
	343 300 deaths
resulting in a net gain of	**19800**

Whole-sale	Retail	Finance property & professional services	Catering	Motor trades	Other services	Total
10 200	23 200	7 500	11 400	6 100	17 100	113 300
8 400	31 000	5 700	13 100	6 500	14 400	115 300
1 800	−7 800	1 800	−1 700	−400	2 700	−2 000
11 600	27 000	7 300	12 000	7 200	18 600	124 800
8 200	30 800	5 700	13 100	6 100	13 400	110 000
3 400	−3 900	1 600	−1 100	1 100	5 200	14 800
12 100	26 600	6 700	12 400	7 600	19 200	125 000
9 600	30 600	6 500	12 900	6 900	16 300	118 000
2 500	−4 000	200	−500	700	2 900	7 000
33 900	76 800	21 500	35 800	20 900	54 900	363 100
26 200	92 400	17 900	39 100	19 500	44 100	343 300
7 700	−15 700	3 600	−3 300	1 400	10 800	19 800

The sectors showing deficits over each of the 3 years were retailing and catering.

Capital

Looking next at the capital of **new companies alone** registered in 1982 and 83; again there are more at the smaller end.

Table 9
Companies registered in Great Britain in 1982 and 1983

	1982		1983	
	Number	Nominal capital £ thous	Number	Nominal capital £ thous
Jan	4 122	45 549	6 224	63 513
Feb	7 698	119 474	7 410	175 932
Mar	8 645	141 787	8 849	98 719
Apr	6 728	94 528	8 412	134 030
May	6 566	52 616		
June	8 800	93 492		
Jul	8 147	214 276		
Aug	5 599	59 282		
Sept	7 660	226 138		
Oct	6 366	88 553		
Nov	8 413	117 791		
Dec	6 912	133 466		
Total	85 656	1 386 952		

Table 10
April, 1983

Nominal capital	Total	Public companies	Private companies
Not exceeding £100	5 367		5 367
Over £100 but under £1 000	52		52
£1 000 but under £10 000	1 983		1 983
£10 000 but under £50 000	684		684
£50 000 but under £100 000	119	2	117
£100 000 but under £1 000 000	174	2	172
£1 000 000 and over	33	2	31
Total number	8 412	6	8 406
	£ thous	£ thous	£ thous
Total amount of nominal capital	134 030	12 950	121 080

Calculating an average capital per company for both Table 9 (1982/83) and Table 10 (April, 1983) it's approximately £16 000. per new company registered.

From the statistics we have looked at in Tables 1 to 10, I feel sure you will agree that small businesses play a key role in our economy.

Some Bolton report conclusions

(i) Ample information is readily available about sources of finance, but surprisingly enough there does seem to be an 'information gap'. Although small firms suffer a number of genuine disabilities, by comparison with larger firms in seeking finance from external sources, most of these disabilities reflect the higher costs of lending in small amounts or the higher risk of lending to small borrowers. They do not result from imperfections in the supply of finance and, indeed, the ability and readiness of the financial institutions to exploit every new legitimate demand for funds is one of the greatest strengths of our financial system. Some 93% of small firms approached the clearing banks as their only source of external finance.

(ii) What is required above all for the health of the small firm sector is an economic and taxation system which will enable individuals to acquire or establish new businesses out of personal resources and to develop these on the base of retained profits. Without this no institutional financing arrangements can preserve the small firm sector.

(iii) Bolton's question 'if you need help, to which of the following would you be most likely to turn?' was answered by 3,740 firms as follows:

Accountant	1,383
Solicitor	561
Bank Manager	543
Chamber of Commerce	496
Trade Association	485
Business consultant	143
CBI	129

(iv) Bolton concluded that the main areas in which small businesses could improve their performance were:

1. *Finance.* Small firms frequently lack knowledge of the appropriate sources of development finance and working capital. They are also unskilled in presenting a financial cast to potential investors and lenders.
2. *Costing and control information.* Cost control is often so poor that management frequently learns of an impending crisis only with the appearance of the annual accounts or following an urgent call from the bank manager. Credit control and stock control information is often inadequate.
3. Other areas of weakness were organization, marketing, information use and retrieval, personnel management, technological change, production scheduling and purchase control. Bolton went on to suggest that if it were possible for the banks to impose as a normal condition for the grant of an overdraft to a firm, the production of regular cash flow statements, or the employment of adequate

estimating and budgetary systems (including age lists of debtors and an analysis of stocks in relation to future production programmes), and if such disciplines came to be recognised as helpful for obtaining bank finance, the efficiency of small firms might be increased.

4. Hence, the bank manager might be able to improve the efficiency of his customers, in their interests and his own. He could help them by pointing out the benefits of regular attention to certain simple indices of the health of a business — the profit/sales ratio, the stocks/turnover ratio, return on capital and so on.

In conclusion of this Chapter, I want to mention that both the Government and the banks took positive steps to give more help to small businesses following the Bolton Report. Details of the developments from both parties are given later in this book — including the 88 schemes publicised of late by the Department of Trade and Industry. Before moving into the topics mentioned; I want to deal firstly with the important area of Financial Planning. How this can help you is discussed in the next Chapter.

2. Financial Planning

Financial planning has become more and more important over recent years due to the increasing competitiveness in the 'market place' *whatever the product* and also the rise in business costs particularly rent and wages. Businessmen and bankers are becoming more aware of the need to improve planning to utilise the business resources to the maximum.

Before we go into planning techniques, it's really essential that you understand basic book-keeping and the significance of the accounts your accountant will prepare each year. (Called Financial Accounts or Audited Accounts.) These are *not* just prepared for the tax inspector and bank manager!

They do in fact paint a picture of your business; albeit historic. If you are not sure about basics I recommend you read the companion book in this guide series called *Accounting for Small Businesses.* It takes you right through from basic entries to operating ratios.

There's really no mystique about financial accounts. One of the problems is the terminology. It's like all trades — whether hi-technology; agriculture or banking; we all use 'jargon' I will try hard not to!

But let's get into an example. Open any set of accounts and the main documents you are looking for are (i) the Trading and Profit and Loss account (ii) the Balance Sheet.

What can we learn from these figures in Table 1? Incidentally, when I look at any business records, I always start with this 'trading' account. To me it paints a picture of a year's activities!

This business generated sales of £64000 in 12 months trading. At what cost? You will see costs are split up. Don't worry about this. Accountants will treat costs in different ways calling them by a number of names.

Variable costs, direct costs, fixed costs, overheads, indirect costs, semi-fixed costs etc. etc.

It really does not matter what you call them — they are all deducted before arriving at the *net* profit of your business. *The important thing is to use the same format each year for comparison purposes.*

Table 1
The trading and profit and loss account of Business 'A' for the year ended 30.6.81

				£	
	Sales			64 000	(a)
less	*cost of sales:*				
	opening stock	Nil	(1.7.80.)		
	plus purchases	80 000			
		80 000			
	less				
	closing stock	45 000	(30.6.81.)		
		35 000		35 000	(b)
	Gross Profit			29 000	(c)
less	*overheads:*				
	rent	10 000			
	wages	6 000			
	finance	2 000			
	sundries + depre'tion	2 000			
		20 000		20 000	(d)
	Net Profit		(before tax)	9000	(e)

What else can we learn about our Business A? The cost of sales was £35000 — let's work that as a percentage:

$$\frac{\text{cost of sales}}{\text{sales}} \times 100$$

$$\frac{(b)}{(a)} \quad \frac{35\,000}{64\,000} \times 100 = 55\%$$

so everything we sell has a cost of 55%
The gross profit is £29 000 and as a percentage:

$$\frac{\text{gross profit}}{\text{sales}} \times 100$$

$$\frac{(c)}{(a)} \quad \frac{29\,000}{64\,000} \times 100 = 45\%$$

it should of course be 45% if you think about it!
so we are saying that our gross profit percentage is 45%. What about overheads?
Let's calculate again:

$$\frac{\text{overheads}}{\text{sales}} \times 100$$

$$\frac{(d)}{(a)} \quad \frac{20\ 000}{64\ 000} \times 100 = 31\%$$

Now it doesn't need an accountant to add our cost percentages i.e. 55% + 31% = 86%
Therefore our bottom line — net profit will be 14%. That is not too bad! I visit many businesses where the net profit is 5% or less!
The percentages we calculated are interesting as a measure of costs to sales but are *far more meaningful* if you compare a series of figures:

Table 2 Business A
Trading and profit and loss account

for the year ended		30.6.81.	30.6.82.	30.6.83.
Sales		64 000	80 000	92 000
less				
cost of sales		35 000	48 400	59 800
Gross profit		29 000	31 600	32 200
less *overheads:*				
rent	10 000			
wages	6 000			
finance	2 000			
*sundries	2 000			
†depreciation	20 000	20 000	27 500	34 000
Net profit/loss (before tax)		9 000	4 100	(loss 1 800)

Now this is not an usual situation. If you asked the businessman *before* June 1983 'how are things going?' he *might* tell you 'fine; *sales are increasing again this year'*.
However as you can see from the figures in Table 2 although sales and the gross profit have increased; the problem is that overhead costs have also increased and the business made a loss in Year 3.
If we calculate the percentages again:

* *Depreciation* — the objective is to write off against profit the cost of a fixed asset over its useful working life. *It does not involve any outflow of cash.*

Table 3

		30.6.81.	30.6.82.	30.6.83.
$\frac{\text{cost of sales}}{\text{sales}}$	× 100	55%	60%	65%
$\frac{\text{gross profit}}{\text{sales}}$	× 100	45%	40%	35%
$\frac{\text{overheads}}{\text{sales}}$	× 100	31%	35%	37%
$\frac{\text{net profit}}{\text{sales}}$	× 100	14%	5%	—

I know this looks an extreme example but you would be surprised how many times this sort of situation occurs! By monitoring the performance percentage figures from your Trading and Profit and Loss account you can be more aware of how your business is performing. Later we will look at forward planning techniques which will link in with this type of analysis.

When the 1982 figures were produced; had the businessman seen the deterioration in the ratios:

Table 4

cost of sales	55%	to	60%
gross profit	45%	to	40%
overheads	31%	to	35%
net profit	14%	to	5%

then perhaps he could have taken some prompt action to avoid the loss made in 1983.

We have not yet mentioned anything about Balance Sheets! As I said earlier I like to start by looking at the trading account to get the picture before turning to the second document in the financial accounts which is the *balance sheet.*

The balance sheet is simply a list of assets and liabilities of the business on *one particular day*. It's a snapshot of the business. Unfortunately many bankers have in the past been obsessed by the balance sheet; paying little regard to the trading accounts. Again of course, there are significant

ratios to be calculated. However both trading **and** balance sheets are important aspects of any business.
The assets are usually split into

current assets:	e.g. stock, debtors, cash
and *fixed assets:*	e.g. plant and machinery; land and buildings

The liabilities are usually split into

current liabilities:	e.g. creditors, bank overdraft
and *term liabilities:*	e.g. mortgage; long-term bank loan

The total of current and fixed assets *less* all liabilities equals the **net worth** of the business. Again terminology can confuse you. It can be known as capital; proprietors' stake; owners investment; equity; surplus or net tangible assets! Let's look at an example to clarify.

Table 5
Business A balance sheet as at 30.6.81

Assets			
Current assets:		£	
Cash			340
Debtors			5 500
Stock			45 000
			50 840
Fixed assets:			
net after depreciation charge	Fixtures/fittings		2 500
	Vehicles		4 500
Total Assets			57 840
less			
Liabilities			
Creditors		22 500	
Bank overdraft		10 300	
		32 800	32 800
		Net worth	**25 040**

The sort of vertical presentation in Table 5 is often seen, but if we re-write it side by side so that both sides 'balance' it looks like this.

Table 6
Business A balance sheet as at 30.6.81

Liabilities	£		**Assets**		
Creditors	22 500		Cash	340	
Bank	10 300		Debtors	5 500	
			Stock	45 000	(e)
	32 800	(b)		50 840	(d)
			Fixture/fittings	2 500	
Capital/Net worth	25 040	(c)	Vehicles	4 500	
	57 840			57 840	(a)

Now you can see why it's called a balance sheet! Whatever you do to one side the other side must be altered by a like amount. Or if we increased, say, debtors, there may well be a reduction in stock. So that both sides will always balance.

Let's examine the figures in Table 6.

1. As at 30.6.81 Business A had total assets of £57840 (a).
2. At the same date the business debts totalled £32800 (b).
3. The net worth of the business is total assets less liabilities a − b = c **or** £57840 − £32800 = £25040 this is the margin between assets and liabilities and in Business A the debts are covered 1.76: 1 which is not a terribly high coverage.
4. The current assets total £50840 (d) of which a considerable amount is stock £45000. (e)
5. The current assets £50840 (d) exceed the current liabilities £32800 (b) which means that debts would be repaid without resorting to the sale of fixed assets.

Don't get confused — remember the trading account shows 12 months' figures; the balance sheet the figures at one day.

Again, there are ratios which we can draw out but this time we will link into the sales figures from Table 1. Refresh your memory from Table 1 that sales totalled £64000.

Linking this into our balance sheet Table 6;

$$\frac{\text{Sales}}{\text{Total assest}} = \frac{£64\ 000}{57\ 840}$$

1.11

in other words we turned total assets over 1.1 times in the year — doesn't sound terribly good does it?

$$\frac{\text{Sales}}{\text{Stock}} = \frac{\text{£}64\ 000}{45\ 000}$$

$$= 1.4$$

again a slow stock turn.

$$\frac{\text{Sales}}{\text{debtors}} = \frac{\text{£}64\ 000}{5\ 500}$$

$$= 11.6$$

that is not too bad.

From Table 1 again	net profit	£9 000
	total assets	£57 840
as a **percentage**	=	**15.5%**

You must be confused by now, so let's set out the inter-relationship of the percentages/ratios in a chart. There are many other relationships but these are the main ones:

Table 7

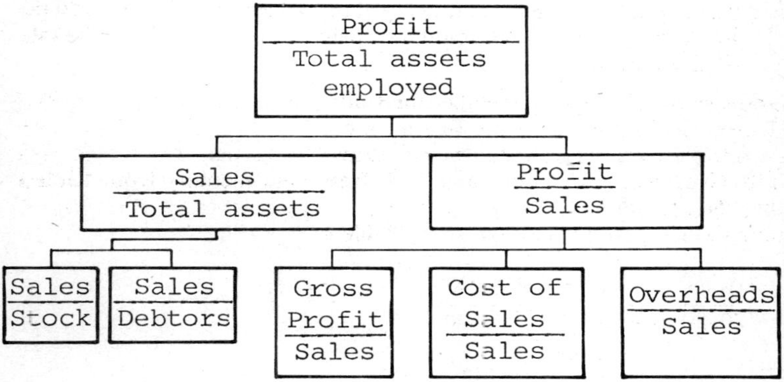

If you now go back through our workings you will see we have calculated all the ones mentioned in Table 7. Also, you will note the trading percentages on the right are interrelated to the ratios on the left. As an example

$$\frac{\text{Profit}}{\text{total assets}} = \frac{\text{Sales}}{\text{total assets}} \times \frac{\text{Profit}}{\text{Sales}}$$

in business A

$$15.5\% = 1.11 \times 14\%$$
$$15.5\% = 15.5\%$$

A series of balance sheets for business A will give us a clearer picture — just as it did with the trading accounts for the 3 years. Here are 3 years' balance sheets for Business A.

Table 8
Business A

Balance sheet as at	30.6.81.	30.6.82.	30.6.83.
		£'s	
Current assets			
cash	340	420	250
debtors	5 500	6 800	7 500
stock	45 000	48 000	49 500
	50 840	55 220	57 250
fixed assets			
fixtures/fittings	2 500	2 500	2 500
vehicles	4 500	4 000	3 500
total assets	57 840	61 720	63 250
less liabilities			
creditors	22 500	22 020	27 750
bank	10 340	12 500	14 500
net worth	25 040	27 200	21 000
for convenience I restate appropriate:			
Sales	64 000	80 000	92 000
Profit	9 000	4 100	(loss 1 800)

Look at the trends:
(i) total assets increasing
but (ii) creditors increasing
and (iii) bank borrowing increasing
and (iv) *net worth* decreasing in year 3
reflecting losses made in year 3
now calculating our ratios:

Table 9
Business A

		30.6.81.	10.6.82.	30.6.83.
Sales / Total assets	(64 000) / (57 840)	1.11	1.29	1.6
Sales / Stock	(64 000) / (45 000)	1.4	1.7	1.85
Sales / Debtors	(64 000) / (5 500)	11.6	11.8	12.2
Net Profit × 100 / Total assets	(9 000) / (57 840)	15.5%	6.6%	– (loss)

The first 3 are acceptable but look at the decline in the net profit/total assets.
Let's look at a comparison of two different businesses X and Y as an illustration:

Table 10

	Business X	Business Y
Profit	£1 000	£400
Sales	£10 000	£5 000
Total assets	£10 000	£2 500
Ratios:		
profit/sales	10%	8%
Profit/Total assets	10%	16%
Sales/Total assets	1	2

You will see that business Y performed better than X with a return on assets employed of 16% although business X had a greater return on sales — 10% as opposed to Y's 8%.

Gearing

You will often hear bank managers and accountants referring to 'gearing'. To a banker this is simply the relationship between total borrowings and net worth. The business is said to be 'highly-geared' when borrowed money is high relative to net worth and 'low-geared' when in the opposite situation. For total borrowings I would include all borrowings irrespective of the length of credit. Include hire purchase and leasing.

Look at the balance sheet of our Business A as at 30.6.81.

Table 11

Liabilities	£		**Assets**	£	
Creditors	22 500		Cash	340	
Bank	10300	(e)	Debtors	5500	
			Stock	45 000	
	32 800	(b)		50 840	(d)
			Fixture/fittings	2 500	
Capital/Net worth	25 040	(c)	Vehicles	4 500	
	57 840			57 840	

This business gearing is e:c (£10300: £25040)
or 0.4: 1 (a low gearing)

The borrowings in this example are only the bank — don't include creditors unless there is part beyond normal trade terms. *Bankers would traditionally view a gearing approaching 1:1 as high.* However, nowadays they will go higher if satisfied with the viability of the proposed project and finance.

The gearing ratio we have looked at should more correctly be referred to as 'capital gearing'. There is another measure called 'income gearing'. You calculate this by looking at past trading records and then later at the *projected trading position*. Look at Business A's past Trading and Profit and Loss Account.

To calculate income gearing the finance costs are looked at relative to profit *before* tax after adding back on any depreciation charge and finance charges.

In our example £2000: £11000

thus the finance costs are well covered. *Bankers would traditionally look for interest cover at least twice over.*
There is however no mathematical formula that would make life easy (but probably boring) — so much will depend on the structure and prospects of the individual business.
By now you are probably terribly confused amidst a mountain of ratios and percentages! Don't worry — in the next chapter we will look at 2 case studies and the approach you should take in dealing with your finance.

Table 12
The Trading and Profit and Loss account of Business 'A' for the year ended 30.6.81.

			£
Sales			**64 000**
less cost of sales:			
opening stock	Nil	(1.7.80.)	
plus purchases	80 000		
	80 000		
less closing stock	45 000	(30.6.81.)	
	35 000		35 000
		Gross Profit	29 000
less overheads:			
rent	10 000		
wages	6 000		
finance	2 000		
sundries + depreciation	2 000		
	20 000		20 000
		Net Profit (before tax)	9 000

Management accounts

So far we have only looked at historic accounts. You will probably have heard people talking about 'management accounting'. This is simply providing management information in an on-going situation; rather than looking backwards to where you have been!

Budgeting: 'a plan for the business looking ahead.'

— do you really need to budget?
— where does finance fit in?
— what can you do to improve your financial management?
— where do we start?

The starting point should be a statement of your business objectives:

What do you really want from your business?

— to make a reasonable living?

— to survive?

— to buy a Rolls Royce?

Your objectives may in fact be very long-term or short-term but I think it is a good way to clarify your thoughts: to set them down on paper. Your objectives will then be reflected in your technical plan (or operational plan) which will include production and sales.

This in turn will affect your business financial plan.

Table 13
Objectives

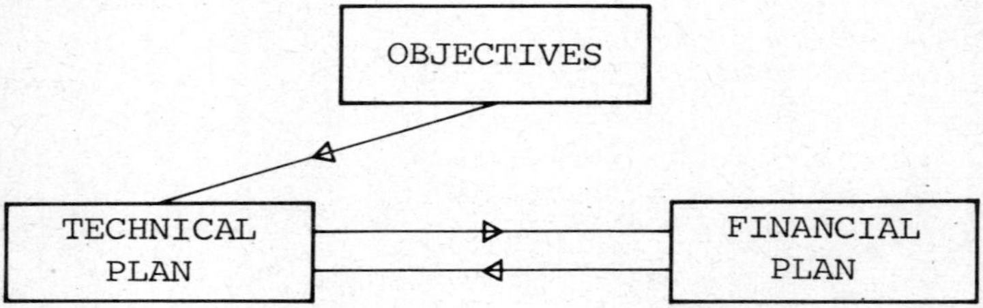

The financial plan will consist of 3 essential parts:

Cash

Capital expenditure

and **Profit**

Table 14
Financial Plan

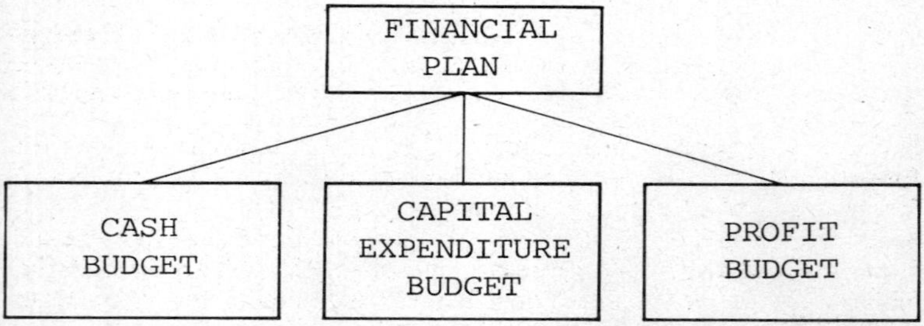

You will see I have now re-introduced the word 'budget'. Many people say they *cannot* budget. I think it's essential to budget! You have really got to know where you are trying to go.

We have discussed the historic trading and profit and loss account — this will help us in *profit* budgeting; as you will shortly see. We have not mentioned **cash**. Don't forget, a business fails when it cannot pay its debts or wages etc. as they fall due. This shortage of **cash** is not necessarily related to a lack of profitability.
Profit may well be an 'opinion'; for example the treatment of depreciation and stock valuations will alter reported profit. However, it is certain that cash flow is a fact.
Before we look at cash planning we will continue on our profit theme — the background work we did with Business A will stand us in a good position. Let's restate the Trading and Profit and Loss Account of Business A in the third year when the loss was made.

Table 15
Business A

			£
Sales			92 000
less cost of sales:			
opening stock	48 000		
plus purchases	61 300		
	109 300		
less closing stock	49 500		
	59 800		59 800
		Gross Profit	32 200
less overheads:			
rent	14 500		
wages	10 000		
finance	3 500		
sundries			
+ depreciation	6 000		
	34 000		34 000
		Loss	1 800

Now in constructing a *profit* budget all we try to do in fact is to project forward our Trading and Profit and Loss account by building up several forecasts and then putting it all together.
With Business A the proprietor will obviously have had the experience of 3 years on which to base his forecast level of sales. In a start-up situation this would be more difficult. You will have to go out and 'test' the market — can you get any firm orders? Who are your main competitors? Is there a place for your product in the market?
With Business A let us say that the projected sales for 1.7.83 to 30.6.84 are £120,000. It's best to further analyse into month and month and we would then schedule:

Table 16
Sales forecast: Business A 1.7.83 to 30.6.84.

	£	(Actual) (Last year)
1983		
July	8 500	6 000
August	9 000	7 000
September	9 500	8 000
October	10 000	8 500
November	12 000	10 200
December	13 500	11 500
1984		
January	6 800	4 700
February	7 500	5 500
March	8 900	7 400
April	10 500	8 200
May	11 960	8 000
June	11 840	7 000
Total	120 000	92 000

Now the next step if you are manufacturing is to consider — have I the production capacity to meet the sales targets? Or in retailing can I purchase sufficient goods to sell? We can now set out a purchases schedule relative to our planned sales:

Table 17
Purchases Forecast Business A 1.7.83 to 30.6.84.

	£	(Actual) (Last Year)
1983		
July	5 300	4 200
August	6 200	5 000
September	6 300	5 300
October	8 000	7 200
November	8 200	7 500
December	9 500	8 200
1984		
January	4 600	4 100
February	5 200	4 000
March	6 200	5 100
April	6 500	5 600
May	7 000	2 100
June	7 000	3 000
Total	80 000	61 300

If you look back at Table 15 you will see that if we make the necessary opening and closing stock entries then we have 'projected' our way to the gross profit figure. Furthermore, if we wanted to we could in fact project our gross profit on a monthly basis.
Now all we have to do is have a crack at the overheads!
The overheads forecast will show the overall costs that will be incurred to achieve the forecast level of sales and of manufacturing; the costs of production. Many overheads may rise if you are trying to increase sales e.g. advertising, wages, postage, telephone, car expenses etc.

Table 18
Overheads Budget

Item	£'s	(Actual) last year)
Rent	14 500	14 500
Wages	11 000	10 000
Finance	4 000	3 500
Sundries + Depreciation	6 000	6 000
	35 500	34 000

We are now ready to put the *profit budget* together, from our work in Tables 16, 17 and 18.
Well that looks better than the previous year's trading when we lost £1800. Let's compare the figures.
You will see that by calculating the ratios of gross profit and overheads to sales it is easy to identify that the projected profit is achieved by increasing sales whilst keeping a tight control of overheads. The gross profit comes out at the same percentage indicating that the cost of sales has remained in direct proportion to the sales. *The profit budget can be split up into 12 separate months if you so wish* This is useful for monitoring purposes which we will look at later in this chapter.
Let's construct a profit budget on that basis for Business A. We already have the sales and purchases figures. The overheads we simply split up into 12 equal months.

Stock valuations

This is an area of difficulty for most businesses *unless* they have few items for valuation or have some form of adequate stock movement records. The stock valuation will have, of course, an effect on the

Table 19
Profit budget for Business A for the period 1.7.83 to 30.6.84

		£'s
Sales		120 000
less cost of sales:		
opening stock*	49 500	
plus purchases	80 000	
	129 500	
less closing stock†	51 000	
	78 500	78 500
	Gross Profit	41 500
less overheads:		
rent	14 500	
wages	11 000	
finance	4 000	
sundries + dep'tion	6 000	
	35 500	35 500
	Net Profit (before tax)	6 000

Table 20
Business A

Actual Trading & Profit & Loss Account 1.7.82 to 30.6.83.	£'s	*Forecast* 1.7.83. 30.6.83 Profit Budget
Sales	92 000	120 000
Gross profit	32 200 (35%)	41 500 (35%)
overheads	34 000 (37%)	35 500 (30%)
net profit (loss)	(1800)	6 000

* actual from closing stock 30.6.83
† estimate

calculated gross profit. However; some businesses will take a "short-cut" by assuming a ratio to calculate the materials consumed in manufacturing or purchases in retailing.

e.g. Sales	£100 000
Assumed Gross Profit Percentage say 50%	£50 000
Hence Materials Consumed	£50 000

The profit budget shows monthly profit and loss figures but the cumulative totals agree with our figures in Table 20. *This profit budget (Table 21) is one of the 2 main budgets which the banks ask for. The other is the cash budget.*
The relationship mentioned of costs rising proportionately to sales leads us into a useful technique called "break-even analysis."

Break-even analysis

This sounds complicated but it really is not!
Again, using business A let's use the forecast profit figures to try to calculate at what point our business breaks-even. In other words — at what point do we make neither profit nor loss?
First we need to separate the costs into 'variable', or 'fixed'. For Business A:
— our variable costs are purchases £80000
— our fixed costs are the list of overheads £35500
Then we graph (see Table 21), fixed costs as a straight line at £35500; variable costs come in on top — starting at £35500 and totalling out at £115500 which of course represents our total costs. Then put in sales starting at zero and ending up at £120000.

This technique like most has its limitations. However it is useful to illustrate the vulnerability or otherwise of a business. The break-even point can be seen and also the 'margin of safety'. ***With our Business A it all looks pretty tight!***
Alternatively break-even can be calculated mathematically by using this formula:

$$\text{Break-even capacity} = \frac{\text{Fixed costs}}{\text{sales less variable costs}} \times 100$$

in our example

$$\text{Break-even capacity} = \frac{35500}{120000 - 80000} \times 100$$

$$= 89\% \text{ of output}$$

Table 21
Business A — Profit Budget for 1.7.83 to 30.6.84.

Net of V.A.T.	1983 July	Aug	Sept	Oct	Nov	Dec
SALES:	8500	9000	9500	10000	12000	13500
less purchases	5300	6200	6300	8000	8200	9500
(increase in stock*	(200)	(300)	(150)	—	(200)	(150)
GROSS PROFIT	3400	3100	3350	2000	4000	4150
less overheads:						
Rent	1208	1208	1208	1208	1208	1208
Wages	916	916	916	916	916	916
Finance	333	333	333	333	333	333
Sundries + depreciation	500	500	500	500	500	500
Overheads total	2957	2957	2957	2957	2957	2957
NET PROFIT	443	143	393	(957)	1043	1193

* Stock valuations: refer to the appropriate section overleaf.

$$\text{Break-even sales} = \frac{\text{Fixed costs} \times \text{sales}}{\text{Sales} - \text{variable costs}}$$

$$= \frac{35500 \times 12000}{120000 - 80000}$$

$$= \frac{35500 \times 12000}{40000}$$

$$= \textbf{£10 650}$$

Also by playing around with the formula you can answer the following *question*:

> 'at what level of sales will the business achieve a net profit of say £10000 — assuming overheads (fixed costs) stay at the same figure?'

1984 Jan	Feb	March	April	May	June	Totals
6800	7500	8900	10500	11960	11840	120000
4600	5200	6200	6500	7000	7000	80000
—	—	(100)	(200)	(200)	—	(1500)
2200	2300	2800	4200	5160	4840	41500
1208	1208	1208	1208	1210	1210	14500
916	916	916	916	920	920	11000
333	333	333	333	335	335	4000
500	500	500	500	500	500	6000
2957	2957	2957	2957	2965	2965	35500
(757)	(657)	(157)	1243	2195	1875	6000

New sales total $= \text{(Fixed Costs + Net Profit)} \times \dfrac{\text{Sales}}{\text{Gross Profit}}$

$$= (35500 + 10000) \times \frac{120000}{40000}$$

$$= \textbf{£136 500}$$

Let's finish off break-even by quickly looking at Business B which shows a vastly different position to Business A.

Assume: Sales	£60 000
variable costs	£20 000
fixed costs	£20 000

Table 22
Break-Even Graph Business A

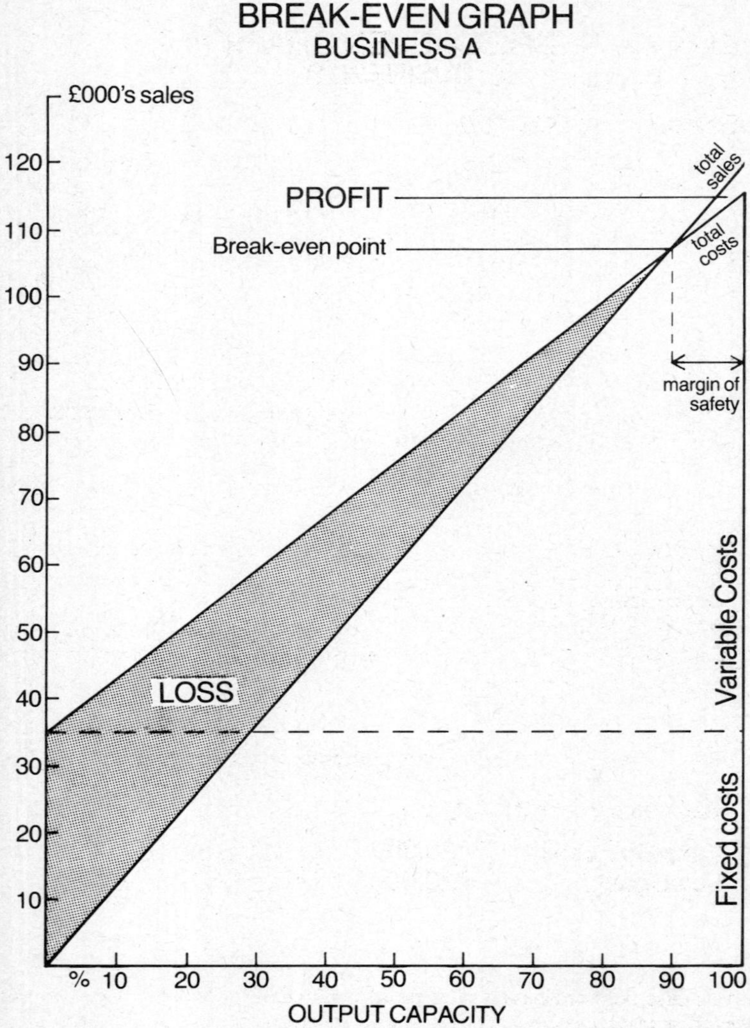

Table 23
Break-Even Graph

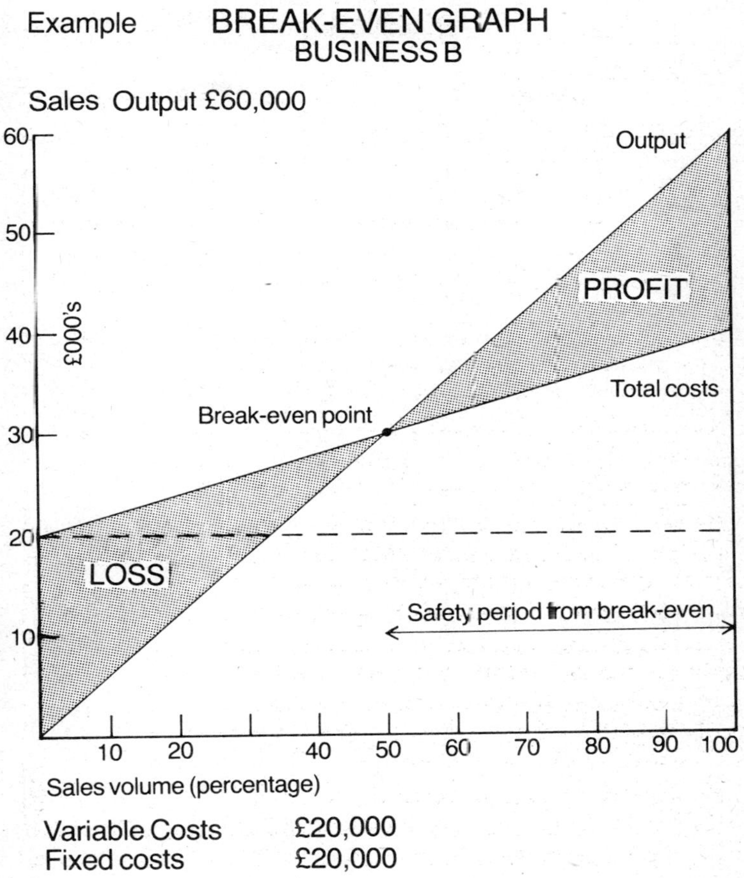

In this case the break-even sales point is reached quickly at £30 000 and there is a good margin of safety. Break-even capacity is 50% output.

Cash budgets

Recalling our 3 essentials in the financial plan:

(i) Profit
(ii) Capital Expenditure
(iii) Cash

We have dealt with, in detail, profit and now we move on to capital expenditure and cash flow.

Whether you are purchasing capital items — such as plant, machinery or paying trading items such as bills due, or wages, they are all cash items. *A cash budget or forecast is therefore simply a statement of expected cash receipts and cash payments over a set period.*

The cause of many business failures is a lack of cash available to meet commitments as they fall due. Wages and creditors *cannot* be paid from profits — they must be paid by cash!

The forecasting of cash movement in your business is essential — it will alert you to action to be taken in good time. Cash is an expensive and scarce commodity. Why not look after it with care?

The cash flow forecast (cash budget) is needed along with your profit budget, when looking for finance. Most bank managers will ask you for a cash flow forecast so they can see the cash flow relative to your business.

Most of the figures are already available in our profit budget. All we need to do is restate the profit budget in cash terms and include also any sale of fixed assets, grants receivable; capital items purchased. The main difference is really one of timing. For example, sales — if sold on credit there will be a delay in receipt of cash. Or purchases — if you take trade credit; payments will not be needed immediately.

Lets start with a capital expenditure budget. Again it's for our Business A.

Table 24
Capital expenditure budget 1.7.83 to 30.6.84

	Date	*Amount*
Planned Purchases:		
Machinery	1.10.83.	£1 500
New Van	1.12.83.	£2 900
	total	£4 400
less *disposals*		
Old van	1.12.83.	500
	Net	£3 900

Now we have to decide on sales and purchases. Let's assume that our Business A receives all cash from sales within the month. We will assume all purchases are paid for in the month following. *These assumptions are obviously very important and will of course differ with different types of trade.*

Now referring to our profit budget (Table 21) and our Capital expenditure budget (Table 24) let's have a go at a Cash Budget, remembering to include VAT in our calculations.
The peak debit balance is shown at £15667 occurring in January 1984. Usually when you have completed the cash flow forecast there is a tendency just to accept that bottom line prediction because it's been such hard work!

Don't!

Can you restructure the cash flow to avoid this high peak? In the case of our Business A, capital expenditure of £2 900 is planned for December 1983. Could this be postponed until spring? This would help take out this peak requirement. The cash forecast also shows total cash in £138 500, cash out £132 400. Hence a positive improvement over the year of £6 100.
A final word in cash management from Mr. Micawber. 'Annual income twenty pounds, annual expenditure nineteen pounds, nineteen shillings and sixpence. Result happiness.
Annual income twenty pounds, annual expenditure twenty pounds and sixpence. Result misery!'
Let's recap at this stage. *We now have our two main budget documents.*
(i) our profit budget
(ii) our cash budget
Both these documents will come into use in the next chapter when we look at two case studies.
You will have noticed by now that certain items appear in the profit budget and *not* the cash budget, and vice versa. Here is a list to clarify.

Profit Budget	*Cash Budget*
Include:	Include:
Invoiced Sales	Sales Receipts
Materials *Used*	Sale of fixed assets
All costs incurred	Capital expenditure
Interest Charges only	Grants
Depreciation	Costs Paid
	Loan/H.P. repayments and Interest
	V.A.T.
	Creditors paid for supplies
Exclude:	Exclude:
Capital expenditure	Depreciation
Grants	
Sale of fixed assets	
Loan/H.P. Capital repayments	
V.A.T.	

Table 25
Cash Flow Forecast For Business 'A'

CASH FLOW FORECAST FOR Business A

RECEIPTS	1983 July	Aug	Sept.	Oct	Nov
Sales Receipts:	8500	9000	9500	10 000	12000
Plus VAT (15%)	1275	1350	1425	1500	1800
Capital Receipts:					
SUB-TOTAL	9775	10350	10925	11500	13800
PAYMENTS					
Purchase Payments:	*3000	5300	6200	6300	8000
plus VAT (15%)	450	795	930	945	1200
Rent					7250
Wages	916	916	916	916	916
Finance			1000		
Sundries (exclude depreciation)			1500		
VAT Settlement			1875		
Capital expenditure				1500	
SUB-TOTAL	4366	7011	12421	9661	17366
NET CASH FLOW (OUTFLOW)	5409	3339	(1496)	1839	(3566)
OPENING	(14500)	(9091)	(5752)	(7248)	(5409)
CLOSING	(9091)	(5752)	(7248)	(5409)	(8975)

* brought forward from JUNE 1983

1/7/83 to 30/6/84

Dec	1984 Jan	Feb	Mar	Apr	May	June	TOTALS
13500	6800	7500	8900	10500	11960	11840	120 000
2025	1020	1125	1335	1575	1794	1776	18 000
500							500
16025	7820	8625	10235	12075	13754	13616	138 500
8200	9500	4600	5200	6200	6500	7000	76000
1230	1425	690	780	930	975	1050	11400
					7250		14500
916	916	916	916	916	920	920	11000
1000			1000			1000	4000
2500			500				4500
1950			585			2190	6600
2900							4400
18696	11841	6206	8981	8046	15645	12160	132 400
(2671)	(4021)	2419	1254	4029	(1891)	(1456)	6100
(8975)	(11646)	(15667)	(13248)	(11994)	(7965)	(9856)	
(11646)	(15667)	(13248)	(11994)	(7965)	(9856)	(8400)	

PEAK DEBIT BALANCE (arrow pointing to Jan (15667))

Control and monitoring

We have spent a lot of time preparing our forecasts for Business A for the year 1.7.83 to 30.6.84. It is not sufficient to put these aside in a drawer! Performance of our business should be monitored against our plans. We can then keep on top of progress and take quick action if we encounter problems.

We can therefore add to our Table 13 both putting plans into practice, and management control and monitoring to look like this.

Table 26

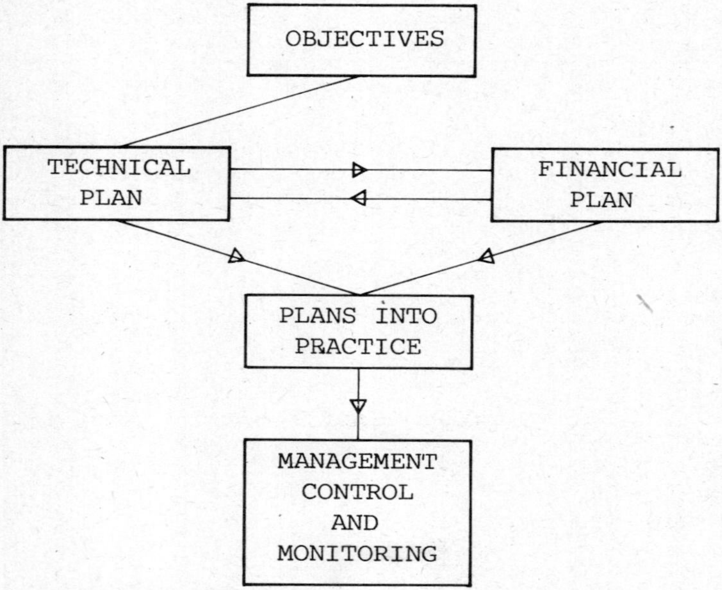

(i) Monitoring cash flow

All we need to do here is to adapt our cash budget to incorporate columns for 'actual' results to be inserted each month alongside the 'budgeted' figures.

(ii) Monitoring overheads

Using a layout as illustrated in Table 27 overheads can be checked on a monthly basis plus a running check on the year to date. These figures are then carried forward into monitoring of the profit budget.

The figures in Table 27 for July budget are simply a copy from our total profit budget (Table 21).

Table 27
Overheads analysis report — Business A (for month ended 31.7.83).

Net of V.A.T.	This Month		Year to Date	
	Budget	Actual	Budget	Actual
Rent	1208			
Wages	916			
Finance	333			
Sundries				
Depreciation	500			
	£2957			

(iii) Monitoring profit
Again looking at our profit budget (Table 21) by drawing in additional columns for each month you could monitor in that way.
An alternative is to use a similar layout to our overheads monitoring form as follows:

Table 28
Profit (loss) Report — Business A (For Month Ended 31.7.83)

Net of V.A.T.	This Month (July)		Cumulative Year to Date	
	Budget	Actual	Budget	Actual
SALES	8500			
less Purchases	5300			
(increase) decrease in stock	(200)			
Gross Profit	**3400**			
LESS Overheads (per overheads report)	2957			
Net Profit (before tax)	**443**			

(iv) Debtor analysis

Table 29
Cash Flow Forecast for Business A

CASH FLOW FORECAST FOR Business A

	BUDGET July	ACTUAL	BUDGET Aug.	AC etc →
RECEIPTS				
Sales	8500			
etc				
etc				
SUB-TOTAL	9775			
PAYMENTS				
Purchases	3000			
etc				
Overheads				
etc				
SUB-TOTAL	4366			
NET CASH FLOW (OUTFLOW)	5409			
OPENING	(14500)			
CLOSING	(9091)			

1/7/83 to 30/6/84

TUAL	BUDGET MAY	ACTUAL	BUDGET JUNE	ACTUAL	ANNUAL TOTALS

Table 30

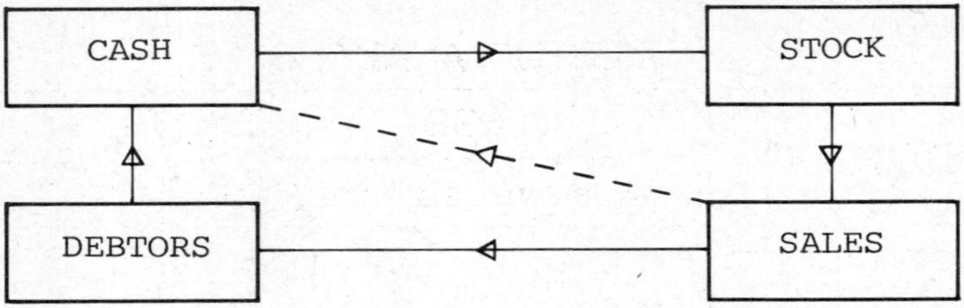

We discussed earlier the management of cash as a scarce commodity. Equally it's important to look after stock which when sold produces in turn either cash or debtors. This is known as the working capital cycle — or at least part of it! Cash is also needed as we discovered earlier to pay bills, wages, etc.
By preparing an analysis of debtors at regular intervals, you can keep a careful watch on slow payers and chase where necessary. A simple way of doing this is illustrated in Table 31 and this is known as an "age-analysis of debtors."

Summary

Let us recall what we have looked at in this chapter using Business A.

1. The trading and profit and loss account.
2. The balance sheet.
3. Some useful ratios and how they are interrelated.
4. Gearing — the relationship of borrowed money to net worth.
5. Budgets — a profit budget.
   — a cash budget.
   — a capital expenditure budget.
6. Break even analysis — how to locate the break-even point and margin of safety.
7. Control and monitoring — some suggested key areas and specimen forms.

All of this work will help as we move into the next chapter considering your approach to the Bank Manager and 2 case studies which we will work through.

Table 31
Debtor Analysis

DEBTOR	AGE				REMARKS
	TOTALS	1 MONTH	2 MONTHS	3 MONTHS AND OVER	
£1000 AND OVER OTHERS					
PERCENTAGES	100%	%	%	%	

3. Preparing a Case for Finance

In the last chapter on financial planning we discussed at length profit budgeting, cash budgeting and other useful planning techniques. In this chapter we will be seeing how you should present your case to the Bank Manager or other financial institution, what he will be looking for and then we will be looking in detail at two case studies.

A poorly presented case to the bank can affect your prospects of obtaining finance! Your presentation should be as clear and concise as possible. In my opinion its always best to give the financier time to study in advance the paperwork which you have prepared. Why not send him the documentation, arrange an appointment and go to see him when he has had a chance to study the figures. Don't forget *you* may well have been thinking about the figures and business details for a matter of days or even months — but if the Bank Manager is confronted by an array of figures it will be a daunting task to try to immediately come to grips with them.

You must be clear on detail in your presentation. The amount of finance required and the period for which it is needed; the purpose for which the finance is sought; the business prospects of the business; the existing finance position of the business and the management structure. I have seen many project presentations totalling some 30 or more pages, but lacking a concise statement about the finance required. Of course it's important to give details about the business, the market place etc. etc. but at the end of the day the financier will be interested in the amount of money you wish to borrow and how you can repay. The detail of the required documentation will vary from whether you are approaching a bank manager for some short-term finance or a finance house for hire purchase or leasing; or equity capital from a merchant bank. You can put together your project details in any order you wish but I offer the following points for your consideration.

I would start by giving details of:

(i) *The business* — brief details of when the business was established, the premises it operates from, how business has developed and grown over the years. The structure of the business — is it a sole proprietor, company or partnership? The share capital position and list of share holders if a company situation.

(ii) *Key management* — the age, experience and qualifications of directors and senior management. If appropriate include an organisational chart for your business. Outline senior management functions and responsibilities.

(iii) *The market place* — what is your business place within the market — do you have a strong or weak product? What is the demand from the market place, is it long or short term? Can you help verify the market place with trade association publications or market research documentation?

Who are your main competitors? — do you have competitive advantages of pricing, location? What are your disadvantages?

Include a description of your products: are they highly technological or simple? I always think it's useful to include product display leaflets or brochures with an indication of the production cost and ultimate selling price.

(iv) For *financial performance* include your last three years audited accounts if available, your up to date figures for debtors, creditors, stock, bank balance, H.P., leasing, other loans, etc.

Give details of previous loan agreements taken and repaid.

(v) *The business plan* In the last chapter we discussed at length how the business objectives would be reflected in the production or technical plan which in turn affects the financial plan. We looked at the financial plan and its constituent parts, the profit budget, capital expenditure budget and cash budget.

Within this presentation, therefore, you should include a brief synopsis of your business plan but include in detail your cash budget, capital expenditure budget and profit budget for the current twelve months.

Also it is worth including a few notes on how you arrived at the assumption made before preparing your budgets. For example the level of sales, product price, terms of trade etc.

(vi) *The amount of money required* — state the amount and type of finance required and when it would be needed. Relate this to the amount of capital (net worth) in your business. Does your request look reasonable?

Does your request include a margin for unforeseen circumstances. In other words is the amount requested sufficient?

The amount requested should tie in with your cash budget mentioned previously.

(vii) *Repayment* — does the projected profit from your profit budget and cash flow from your cash flow forecast, indicate feasibility of your repayment plans? How quickly will you be able to generate repayment. Should you try and negotiate a 'holiday' as regards loan repayments for say 12 months?

Remembering our 'break-even' analysis in the previous chapter. Have you included a statement of the level of output at which will you reach break-even point? I think this is most important as it illustrates the vulnerability or otherwise of your projected sales plan. This point is often overlooked.

(viii) *Security* — this area will probably be open to negotiation between you and your bank manager but it is always worth giving an indication of what you have in mind. It's worth detailing what assets there are and will be available as security. Are any assets already pledged for security for other loans?

(ix) *Structuring the finance* — in the next chapter on sources of finance we look in detail at short-term, medium-term, long-term finance and other alternative means of finance. It's just worth mentioning briefly here that within your presentation to the bank you should bear in mind that **a** if you are requiring working capital, bridging finance, finance for short lived assets you probably require *short-term finance*. **b** If you require finance to purchase assets with a medium-term life, for example plant and machinery, you will require *medium-term finance*. **c** If you require finance for the purchase of longer term assets e.g. buildings, land, you will require *long-term finance*. **d** If you require finance to develop your exporting and finance of foreign trade you will require *export finance*.

Finally make your approach to the bank in plenty of time particularly if you are looking for long-term finance. If you ask the Bank Manager to make a hasty decision the answer could well be 'no!'

Case Study No. 1. David Allen Limited

Background

For many years David Allen ran a successful business as a retailer of high class glass and chinaware. He operated four shops in the South East of England, three of which were in small towns and one on the coast at a busy summer holiday centre.

Each shop was run by an individual manager with Mr. Allen directing overall operations. All the businesses were from rented premises. Early in 1983 Mr. Allen suffered a stroke and retired from business.

Control of the business then passed to his son Charles who had recently completed a business studies course at a local college. Charles knew that his father had not had any formal management/financial training and had basically run the business using his experience in the trade and what he described as a feeling for the way things were going. Charles decided however that he must start as though he were purchasing the business and made an appraisal of the situation as he found it.

He knew that his father had not been too pleased in recent months with the way things were going at the shops and he had had several meetings with the Bank Manager concerning the overdraft facility.

Financial Accounts

Table 1

Financial Accounts for the previous three years showed: Trading Results:

Year ended	31.1.80.	31.1.81.	31.1.82.
Sales	185 321	200 471	225 458
Gross Profit	89 139	94 822	104 887
Gross Profit %	48.1%	47.3%	46.5%
Overheads	81 100	88 522	102 207
% of Sales	43.7%	44.1%	45.3%
Net Profit/(Loss)	8 039	6 300	2 680

The Balance Sheet as at 31.1.82. showed the following position.

Comment

The Trading results for the three years to January, 1982 looked satisfactory at first glance. However on closer examination:

1. Sales had hardly kept pace with inflation running through that period and had shown little real growth.
2. Profit margins were slowly falling away as was shown when the gross profit percentages were compared.
3. Overheads were increasing.

Table 2

Liabilities		Assets	
Creditors	16 977	Stock	97 990
Bank	21 968	Debtors	4 940
		Cash in hand	376
Current Liabilities	38 945	Current Assets	103 306
Issued Capital	25 000		
Profit & Loss Account Balance	60 668	Fixed Assets	14 907
		Goodwill	6 400
	124 613		124 613

4. Profitability was falling away and it was over a year since the last figures were extracted.
5. The balance sheet however looked fairly strong with a good measure of liquidity, that is, the amount the current assets exceed the current liabilities. Also there was a sound 'net worth' base.

Due to the historic nature of the figures it was imperative for Charles to know the up to date situation and he called in the company's accountant to audit the books for the year to the end of 31st January, 1983. Meanwhile several creditors were pressing for payment and it was necessary to renegotiate an overdraft facility of £62000 at the Bank, based on the long established track record of the business in order to keep the creditors happy.

In July, 1983 Charles received the following summary of Trading for the year ended 31st January, 1983.

Table 3
Trading and Profit and Loss Account for the 12 month period ending on 31.1.83

Sales	£228 578
Gross Profit	£96 688
Gross Profit %	42.3%
less	
Overheads	£124 242
% of Sales	54.3%
Loss on Trading	(27 554)

Table 4
A summarised Balance Sheet as at the 31.1.83 showed:

Liabilities			Assets	
Creditors		48 191	Stock	119 144
Bank		44 000	Debtors	8 495
			Cash in hand	566
		92 191		128 205
Issued Capital		25 000	Fixed Assets	15 700
Profit & Loss A/C			Goodwill	6 400
Brought forward:	60 668			
less loss	27 554			
	33 114	33 114		
		150 305		150 305

Comment
The Trading Account revealed a loss of £27,554 and bearing in mind these are the figures at the end of January, 1983 they were already out of date. It was likely that further monies had been lost in the first six months of trading in 1983. Charles was therefore very worried about the position and asked the accountant to begin with preparation of figures to bring him right up to date i.e. from the 1st January, 1983 to 30 June, 1983. Looking at the Balance Sheet figures in Table 4, stock had increased together with a rising bank overdraft and creditor position compared with the previous year in Table 2. Sales as shown in Table 3 had increased only marginally to £228,000 which together with a reduced gross profit percentage and rising overhead costs meant a loss in trading in the year of £27,554. Charles was, of course, worried, as any further losses would further deteriorate the net worth of the business. So pending interim accounts Charles decided to visit immediately each shop in turn with the following points in mind.

1. Premises — site and tenure, location, suitability for future development.
2. Management — experience, age and responsibility, general staffing.
3. Market — what was the local competition and could he compete both on price and quality?
4. Products — were they satisfying customers needs?

5. Costing and pricing — how were the prices of the products arrived at? Did each manager keep individual records of costs in the shops?
6. Stock control — was it adequate?
7. Trading Performance — sales — cost of sales — overheads — profitability?

Interim Accounts

The accountant produced interim accounts for the first six months of 1983 which showed the following position.

Table 5

Sales	£108 350
Gross Profit	46 870
Gross Profit %	43%
less	
Overheads	65 010
% of Sales	60%
Loss of Trading	(£18 140)

The Balance Sheet showed:

Table 6

30.6.83.

Liabilities				Assets	
Creditors			66 837	Stock	124 306
Bank			45 070	Debtors	6 421
			111 907		130 727
Issued capital		25 000			
P&L A/C	33 110			Fixed Assets	14 750
less				Goodwill	6 400
loss	18 140	14 970	39 970		
			151 877		151 877

Armed with these further, more up to date figures, Charles immediately called a meeting of all the shop managers, at which his accountant agreed to be present, to explain the results of the first six months of 1983. The shop managers were obviously concerned at the changing pattern of results from those that had been experienced over previous years. They gave Charles the explanation that demand had fallen away from the company's traditionally high-class merchandise and it was decided from the meeting to extend the range of merchandise to include some cheaper product lines. Also, in view of the high stock position at many of the shops, sales would be held with the aim of generating cash to allow Charles to pay pressing creditors and to reduce the amount of borrowed money in the business. Charles reviewed the trading worth of shops with his accountant and it was decided:

1. The development of a new town shopping centre precinct had left one shop losing a substantial catchment area, however the shop manager still saw potential in the site and a deal was agreed whereby the shop manager could purchase the on-going business from Charles.
2. An outlying shop in a market town was making little contribution to sales and plans were made to hive off the business when the shop manager retired very shortly.

Charles felt that the two remaining shops were well sited and had good enthusiastic managers. Based on this rationalisation scheme, in conjunction with his accountant, Charles prepared a profit budget and cash budget for the coming year. He carefully made a note of the assumptions on which his budget was to be based. He began by preparing a sales budget for both shops in conjunction with the two shop managers. Sales were estimated to total £63,500 for shop 'A' and £69,000 for shop 'B' giving total sales of £132,500.

Table 7
Sales Budget July 1983 to June 1984

	July	Aug.	Sept.	Oct.	Nov.	Dec.
Town Shop 'A'	5700	4500	4750	5000	4000	1100
Coast Shop 'B'	10000	8500	7000	3000	3000	6000
	15700	13000	11750	8000	7000	17000

	Jan.	Feb.	Mar.	Apr.	May	June	Total
Town Shop 'A'	3300	3750	4600	6700	5000	5200	63500
Coast Shop 'B'	3000	3500	4500	5000	7000	8500	69000
	6300	7250	9100	11700	12000	13700	132500

He then prepared the associated overheads budget for each shop, plus an overheads charge for the administration of the business (See Table 8).

Table 8
Overheads Budget July 1983 to June 1984

Net of V.A.T. 12 Months

	Town Shop 'A'	Coast Shop 'B'	Administration	Total
Wages and N.I.C.	8152	10100		18252
Casual Wages	2000	4000	—	6000
Rent and Rates	3500	4100	—	7600
Heat and Light	750	850	—	1600
Insurances	—	—	1250	1250
Motor Expenses	—	—	2448	2448
Telephone Charges	170	180	—	350
Repairs and Renewals	500	496	—	996
Printing Stationery, Adverts and Postage	250	250	100	600
Bank Charges & Interest	—	—	4315	4315
Audit & Accountancy	—	—	1250	1250
H.P. Interest	—	—	—	—
Professional charges	—	—	100	100
Sundry Expenses	150	150	—	300
Depreciation Motor Vehicles & Equipment	250	250	2500	3000
Directors Renumeration	—	—	5004	5004
Totals	15 722	20 376	16 967	53 065

Using the data base of sales in Table 7 purchases were forecast to meet these sales needs and then the figures were all amalgamated in a profit budget for the re-structured business. (See Table 9).

Table 9
Profit Budget (after rationalisation scheme)

	1983 July	Aug.	Sept.	Oct.	Nov.	Dec.
Shop Sales	15700	13000	11750	8000	7000	17000
Forecast Sales	15700	13000	11750	8000	7000	17000
Less						
Forecast Purchases	8949	7410	6698	4560	3990	9690
Total Direct Costs	8949	7410	6698	4560	3990	9690
Gross Profit	6751	5590	5053	3440	3010	7310
Less						
Wages & N.I.	1521	1521	1521	1521	1521	1521
Casual wages	500	500	500	500	500	500
Rent and Rates	633	633	633	633	633	633
Heat and Light	133	133	133	133	133	133
Insurances	104	104	104	104	104	104
Motor Expenses	204	204	204	204	204	204
Telephone	29	29	29	29	29	29
Repairs & Renewal	83	83	83	83	83	83
Stationery/ Advertising	50	50	50	50	50	50
Bank Charges	0	0	50	0	0	50
Audit and Acc'tancy	104	104	104	104	104	104
Pro'sional Charges	8	8	8	8	8	8
Sundries	25	25	25	25	25	25
Directors Remun.	417	417	417	417	417	417
Monthly Interest	332	366	329	344	353	347
Trading Profit	2607	1411	861	– 716	– 1156	3101
Less						
Depre'tion	250	250	250	250	250	250
Net Profit/Loss	**2357**	**1161**	**611**	**– 966**	**– 1406**	**2851**

Jan.	Feb.	March.	April	May	1984 June	Years Total
6300	7250	9100	11700	12000	13700	132500
6300	7250	9100	11700	12000	13700	132500
3591	4133	5187	6669	6840	7809	75525
3591	4133	5187	6669	6840	7809	75525
2709	3118	3913	5031	5160	5891	56975
1521	1521	1521	1521	1521	1521	18252
500	500	500	500	500	500	6000
633	633	633	633	633	633	7600
133	133	133	133	133	133	1600
104	104	104	104	104	104	1250
204	204	204	204	204	204	2448
29	29	29	29	29	29	350
83	83	83	83	83	83	996
50	50	50	50	50	50	600
0	0	50	0	0	50	200
104	104	104	104	104	104	1250
8	8	8	8	8	8	100
25	25	25	25	25	25	300
417	417	417	417	417	417	5004
349	339	336	355	349	318	4115
– 1452	– 1034	– 286	863	999	1711	6910
250	250	250	250	250	250	3000
– 1702	**– 1284**	**– 536**	**613**	**749**	**1461**	**3910**

Table 10
Cash Budget (after rationalisation scheme)

	July	Aug.	Sept.	Oct.	Nov.	Dec.
Sales receipts	6000	18055	14950	13513	9200	8050
Total Receipts	6000	18055	14950	13513	9200	8050
Purchase payments	10025	10291	8522	7702	5244	4589
Wages & N.I.	1521	1521	1521	1521	1521	1521
Casual Wages	500	500	500	500	500	500
Rent and Rates	1900	0	0	1900	0	0
Heat and Light	0	0	300	0	0	500
Insurance	0	0	1250	0	0	0
Motor Expenses	204	204	204	204	204	204
Telephone	0	85	0	0	85	0
Repairs and Renewal	83	83	83	83	83	83
Stationery/ Advertising	50	50	50	50	50	50
Bank Charges	0	0	50	0	0	50
Audit and Acc'tancy	0	0	0	1250	0	0
Pro'sional Charges	0	0	0	50	0	0
Sundries	25	25	25	25	25	25
Directors Remun.	417	417	417	417	417	417
Overdraft Interest	0	0	1026	0	0	1044
V.A.T.	2500	0	0	2069	0	0
Total Payments	17225	13176	13948	16311	8129	8982
Net Cash Flow	−11225	4879	1002	−2799	1071	−932
Opening Bank Balance	−25000	−36225	−31346	−30344	−33143	−32072
Closing Bank Balance	−36225 (peak balance)	−31346	−30344	−33143	−32072	−33004

Jan.	Feb.	March	Apr.	May	June	Year's Total
19550	7245	8338	10465	13455	13800	142620
19550	7245	8338	10465	13455	13800	142620
11144	4103	4752	5965	7669	7866	87898
1521	1521	1521	1521	1521	1521	18252
500	500	500	500	500	500	6000
1900	0	0	1900	0	0	7600
0	0	500	0	0	300	1600
0	0	0	0	0	0	1250
204	204	204	204	204	204	2448
0	90	0	0	90	0	350
83	83	83	83	83	83	996
50	50	50	50	50	50	600
0	0	50	0	0	50	200
0	0	0	0	0	0	1250
0	0	0	50	0	0	100
25	25	25	25	25	25	300
417	417	417	417	417	417	5004
0	0	1023	0	0	1022	4115
2064	0	0	1461	0	0	8634
17908	7020	9126	12176	10559	12038	146598
1642	225	– 788	– 1711	2896	1762	– 3978
– 33004	– 31362	– 31136	– 31924	– 33635	– 30740	
– 31362	– 31136	– 31924	– 33635	– 30740	– 28978	

On examination of the figures in the profit budget a forecast annual profit of £3,910 was disclosed. Using this profit budget as a base and having due regard for the timing of payments and purchases a cash budget was produced for the same period (see Table 10) and this indicated a peak bank borrowing requirement of £36,225 (for the rationalised business).
This peak bank facility was agreed by the Bank Manager on the basis that the disposal of the two shops would reduce the bank balance to that shown within the cash flow i.e. an opening balance of £25,000 in July.

Conclusion

The hiving down or rationalisation of any business is always a difficult step to take. Charles saw this action as the only way out of the dilemma in which he was in. There may have been other ways, such as an injection of new monies into the business from an outside investor. Who knows? However he did manage to return the business, albeit in a restructured form, to profitable trading.
I believe that this case clearly illustrates the need to keep up to date as much as possible in monitoring the financial progress of any business. If the problems had been seen earlier perhaps there would have been no need to dispose of the two shops.

Case Study 2 — Peter Smith

Peter Smith aged 34 was employed as a foreman of a large company manufacturing kitchen and bedroom furniture. The company ran into difficulties and Peter Smith was made redundant.
He knew the manufacturing side of the business well and he had made similar items of furniture for friends on a private basis in his garage at home. This had led to other orders which he had not been able to fulfil. With his redundancy payment of £5000 he decided to look into the possibility of setting up his own business. He knew there were suitable premises available in the area and that he would not have too much difficulty in finding some skilled employees.

The project
Smith decided to discuss the project in detail with a local accountant to whom he had been recommended.

(i) *Products*

Smith gave consideration to the product range and decided that initially he would manufacture bedside cabinets, chests of drawers and wardrobes. All these products to be in standard sizes. From experience he knew that the bedside cabinets took half an hour to produce whilst the chest of drawers took one hour each and the wardrobes two hours each. He knew that the material content of the units would cost approximately 40% of the usual selling price. He decided therefore that he could regard the manufacturing times for each unit as standard production times to which he could attach the wage costs of employees. Also he knew the going rate in the industry was £2.50 per hour.

Table 1

Products	Bedside Cabinets	Chest of Drawers	Wardrobes
Selling Price	£5	£13	£32.50
Material Content per unit (40% of Selling Price)	£2	£5.20	£13.00
Standard Production Time	$\frac{1}{2}$ hr.	1 hr.	2 hrs.
Labour Cost (£2.50 per hr.)	£1.25	£2.50	£5.00

(ii) *Sales Forecast*

Again, based on experience and after carrying out some market research Smith gave thought to the likely number of sales he could achieve. An agent friend confirmed that if Smith could manufacture 145 units per week he would be able to sell through established retail outlets with whom he had dealings.

The units targeted would be 40 bedside cabinets, 80 chests of drawers, 25 wardrobes, total 145 units per week.

This would involve production time of:

Table 2

40 × ½ hour	=	20 hours
80 × 1 hour	=	80 hours
25 × 2 hours	=	50 hours
		150 hours

Smith knew that on the basis of a 40 hour production week per person he would need at least three employees, with himself helping out at times during the week.

(iii) *Financial requirements*

As mentioned earlier Smith had a payment of £5000 from his redundancy money plus his car worth £4000. Smith thought he would require other finance but how much and how he would obtain it he was not sure.

The accountant explained that many banks had special schemes aimed at the financing of new businesses but before lending money they liked to ensure that a project had been carefully thought out. Also that the best method of approach was to prepare a business plan setting out in as much detail as possible, the areas that had been considered and the assumptions behind the figure work.

The accountant suggested the following areas for discussion.

(iv) *Business plan check list* — Objectives — Management — Market — Products — Suppliers — Physical Resources — Personnel — Profit and Cash Forecasts — Outside Finance Requirement.

Table 3

Sales — Weekly		£'s
40 Bedside cabinets at £5.00 each	=	200.00
80 Chests of drawers at £13.00 each	=	1040.00
25 Wardrobes at £32.50 each	=	812.50
Total Sales (Net of V.A.T.)		2052.50
less		
Material Cost	£'s	
40 Bedside cabinets at £2.00 each	80	
80 Chests of drawers at £5.20 each	416	
25 Wardrobes at £13.00 each	325	
	821	
Wages Cost	£'s	
40 Bedside cabinets at £1.25 each	50	
80 Chests of drawers at £2.50 each	200	
25 Wardrobes at £5.00 each	125	
	375	
Cost of sales		1196.00
Gross Profit		856.50
Gross Profit %		41.7%

(v) *Profitability* — On the basis of sales of 145 units per week the figures were now extended to give weekly totals.

This showed a gross profit of £856 per week (41.7%). The accountant explained to Smith that so far they had been looking at the variable costs in manufacturing i.e. those costs which vary with the level of activity seen. Clearly, if more production was generated then both wages and material content would be higher in direct proportion to the level of sales. Smith and the accountant then continued their discussion with the other costs of running the business, the overheads, this time multiplying the figures out for the coming twelve months.

(vi) *The overheads budget for 12 months*

Table 4
The Overheads Budget

(Net of V.A.T.)	£
Rent and Rates	4440
Light and Heat	609
Telephone and Postage	320
Administration Wages and N.I.	2580
Drivers Wages	4200
Motor Expenses/Travelling	3120
Insurances	1475
Repairs and Renewals	600
Accountancy/Professional Charges	1200
Adverts/Stationery	340
Leasing Charge (Machine)	1980
H.P. Interest	636
Vehicle Hire	3000
Bank Commission Charge	200
Bank Interest	931
Sundries	744
Depreciation	2256
Proprietor Withdrawals	7500
	36 131

As shown the total overheads anticipated for the 12 months would be £36131.

(vii) *Capital expenditure*
Bearing in mind that expenditure would be needed on wood-working machinery, and a delivery vehicle, Smith decided to hire a vehicle on monthly contract and this would save an outlay of cash.
Machinery would cost £7000 and £5000 of this could be purchased by hire purchase finance, Smith would be required to find a deposit of 15% of the purchase price (£750) with the capital sum and interest charges repayable over three years. The remaining £2000 could be taken by way of a short term leasing agreement at a cost of £165 per month.

(viii) *Break-even level*
Smith and the accountant then calculated a projected break-even level of sales to cover material wages and overhead costs.

Table 5

	£
Sales (Net of V.A.T.)	86 645
Gross Profit @ 41.7%	36 131
less	
Overheads	36 131
Profit/(Loss)	NIL

The figures indicate a break even level of £86 645 worth of sales required before neither profit nor loss would be encountered by the business over the coming 12 months.

(ix) *The profit budget*
Now working with all the previous figures and building up sales and purchases on an annual basis a total sales income of £98 544 was forecast with a gross profit of £41 136 and the resulting net profit of £5 005 after a depreciation charge of £2 256 — see Profit Budget 'A'.

(x) *Cash budget*
Smith felt that on average he would receive the proceeds of sale within 55 days after invoice while he would have to pay for materials within 30 days of invoice. Having due regard for these credit timings a cash budget was prepared on this basis after allowing for the introduction of Smith's capital and the payment of the deposit on the machine to be financed through Hire Purchase.
The cash budget showed a peak bank requirement of £10 751. This occured in Month 4 of the operating year and to allow for a little lee-way the accountant suggested seeking a bank overdraft of £11 000, based on the cash flow figures.

(xi) *Approach for finance*
The assumptions and figures were then all drawn together to formulate a business plan for presentation to his Bank Manager for his consideration. It was decided that the Bank Manager would probably want a little time to consider the figures and therefore Smith called at the bank by appointment and left the business plan with the Manager for his consideration.
At a subsequent meeting a week later the Bank Manager raised several points that he felt were not clear and would require further consideration. *In particular the Bank Manager felt that confirmation of the likely level of sales should be obtained as the level of sales required at £86 645 to achieve the agreed break even situation seemed considerable.* Later, after further discussion and verification of several points the Bank Manager agreed to provide the finance required, i.e. £11 000 by way of overdraft and the business was set up.

Profit Budget A

	1 Jan.	2 Feb.	3 Mar.	4 Apr.	5 May.
Sales	8212	8212	8212	8212	8212
Forecast Sales	8212	8212	8212	8212	8212
Less					
Materials	3284	3284	3284	3284	3284
Manufacturing Wages	1500	1500	1500	1500	1500
Total direct costs	4784	4784	4784	4784	4784
Gross Profit	3428	3428	3428	3428	3428
Less					
Rent & Rates	370	370	370	370	370
Light & Heat	51	51	51	51	51
Telephone & Postage	27	27	27	27	27
Admin Wages	215	215	215	215	215
Drivers Wages	350	350	350	350	350
Motor Exs./Travel	260	260	260	260	260
Insurances	123	123	123	123	123
Repairs & Renewal	50	50	50	50	50
Accountancy/Prof	100	100	100	100	100
Adverts/Stationery	28	28	28	28	28
Machine Lease	165	165	165	165	165
H.P. Interest	53	53	53	53	53
Vehicle Hire	250	250	250	250	250
Bank Charges	17	17	17	17	17
Sundries	62	62	62	62	62
Proprietors withdrawals	625	625	625	625	625
Monthly Interest	26	83	105	107	106
Trading Profit	657	599	577	575	577
Less					
Deprn. M.V./Plant	188	188	188	188	188
Net Profit/Loss	469	411	389	387	389

6 Jun. 8212	7 Jul. 8212	8 Aug. 8212	9 Sep. 8212	10 Oct. 8212	11 Nov. 8212	12 Dec. 8212	Years Total 98544
8212	8212	8212	8212	8212	8212	8212	98544
3284	3284	3284	3284	3284	3284	3284	39408
1500	1500	1500	1500	1500	1500	1500	18000
4784	4784	4784	4784	4784	4784	4784	57408
3428	3428	3428	3428	3428	3428	3428	41136
370	370	370	370	370	370	370	4440
51	51	51	51	51	51	51	609
27	27	27	27	27	27	27	320
215	215	215	215	215	215	215	2580
350	350	350	350	350	350	350	4200
260	260	260	260	260	260	260	3120
123	123	123	123	123	123	123	1475
50	50	50	50	50	50	50	600
100	100	100	100	100	100	100	1200
28	28	28	28	28	28	28	340
165	165	165	165	165	165	165	1980
53	53	53	53	53	53	53	636
250	250	250	250	250	250	250	3000
17	17	17	17	17	17	17	200
62	62	62	62	62	62	62	744
625	625	625	625	625	625	625	7500
85	88	86	65	68	66	46	931
598	595	597	617	615	617	637	7261
188	188	188	188	188	188	188	2256
410	407	409	429	427	429	449	5005

Cash Flow — Cash Budget B

	1 Jan.	2 Feb.	3 Mar.	4 Apr.	5 May
Sales Receipts 1	0	1574	9444	9444	9444
Capital Introduced	5000	0	0	0	0
Total Receipts	5000	1574	9444	9444	9444
Materials	3284	3284	3284	3284	3284
Manufacturing Wages	1500	1500	1500	1500	1500
Rent & Rates	370	370	370	370	370
Light & Heat	0	0	155	0	0
Telephone & Postage	5	5	70	5	5
Admin Wages	215	215	215	215	215
Drivers Wages	350	350	350	350	350
Motor Exs./Travel	260	260	260	260	260
Insurances	1475	0	0	0	0
Repairs & Renewal	50	50	50	50	50
Accountancy/Prof	100	100	100	100	100
Adverts/Stationery	120	20	20	20	20
Machine Lease	165	165	165	165	165
H.P. Interest	53	53	53	53	53
Vehicle Hire	250	250	250	250	250
Bank Charges	0	0	50	0	0
Sundries	62	62	62	62	62
Proprietors withdrawals	625	625	625	625	625
Overdraft Interest	0	0	214	0	0
Machine Deposit	750	0	0	0	0
VAT	0	0	0	3695	0
H.P. Capital	118	118	118	118	118
Total Payments	9752	7427	7911	11122	7427
Net Cash Flow	–4752	–5853	1532	–1670	2017
Opening Bank Balance	0	–4752	–10605	–9073	–10751
Closing Bank Balance	–4752	–10605	–9073	–10751	–8734

6	7	8	9	10	11	12	Years
Jun.	Jul.	Aug.	Sep.	Oct.	Nov.	Dec.	Total
9444	9444	9444	9444	9444	9444	9444	96012
0	0	0	0	0	0	0	5000
9444	9444	9444	9444	9444	9444	9444	101012
3284	3284	3284	3284	3284	3284	3284	39408
1500	1500	1500	1500	1500	1500	1500	18000
370	370	370	370	370	370	370	4440
129	0	0	150	0	0	175	609
70	5	5	70	5	5	70	320
215	215	215	215	215	215	215	2580
350	350	350	350	350	350	350	4200
260	260	260	260	260	260	260	3120
0	0	0	0	0	0	0	1475
50	50	50	50	50	50	50	600
100	100	100	100	100	100	100	1200
20	20	20	20	20	20	20	340
165	165	165	165	165	165	165	1980
53	53	53	53	53	53	53	636
250	250	250	250	250	250	250	3000
50	0	0	50	0	0	50	200
62	62	62	62	62	62	62	744
625	625	625	625	625	625	625	7500
298	0	0	239	0	0	179	931
0	0	0	0	0	0	0	750
0	3695	0	0	3695	0	0	11086
118	118	118	118	118	118	118	1416
7969	11122	7427	7931	11122	7427	7896	104535
1475	−1679	2017	1513	−1679	2017	1548	−3523
−8734	−7260	−8938	−6921	−5409	−7089	−5070	
−7260	−8938	−6921	−5409	−7087	−5070	−3523	

Conclusion

Start-up finance is always difficult to obtain as there is no 'track-record' for the business. Verification of likely sales levels is always very important and sometimes crucial to the business survival. In chapter 5 we look in more detail at this aspect and the associated problems of high break-even levels.

In both case studies we have looked at *there is a need for management information*, particularly profit and cash budgeting. In the next chapter we will look at the sources of finance available to help the businessman.

4. Sources of Finance

The bank's response

We discussed earlier the comments of the Bolton report. Perhaps Mark Twain's observation on banking was near the mark:
'A banker — a person who lends you his umbrella when the sun shines but wants it back when it begins to rain'
However, it's true to say that in recent years there has been growing recognition of the major contribution that small firms can make to the economy, and the banks, for their part, have been actively seeking to increase their support to the small firms sector. The London clearing banks are Barclays, Lloyds, Midland, National Westminster (together with its subsidiary, Coutts) and Williams and Glyn's. The Scottish clearing banks are Bank of Scotland, Clydesdale Bank and Royal Bank of Scotland.
Virtually all small firms operate an account at one of the clearing banks: as a result, the banks are the main — and in many cases the only — point of contact that small firms have with the financial system. In the past few years, the banks have developed a large number of schemes and facilities to supplement their traditional services for small firms. They now have a wide range to offer to the small business customer. In some cases different banks have chosen to pursue different paths, individual banks have launched particularly distinctive services, which I will detail later.
The banks' services have attracted considerable interest and have helped to demonstrate the banks' responsiveness to the financial needs of their business customers. The major part of the banks' support for small firms continues to take the form of overdrafts and loans, managerial advice and other traditional banking services. This may well be all that is required.
A recent survey indicated that in the six months October 1981–April 1982 the clearing banks extended over a quarter of a million new facilities (including increases in existing facilities) to small firms, amounting to a total of about £2.8 billion. It should also be remembered that many firms have little need to turn to their banks for finance.
The clearing bank overdraft remains the most versatile form of finance available to the business customer. Within limits, the amount borrowed can fluctuate in response to the flow of cash passing through the customer's account. Interest is charged on each day's outstanding balance. The overdraft is cheaper than any other form of external finance (depending on the taxation situation).

Overdrafts are intended to cover short-term borrowing, to finance stock and work in progress. The sale of the finished product will generate the funds for repaying the borrowing. However, an increasing proportion of overdraft lending has taken on a 'hard core' quality and many firms operate their accounts permanently with an overdrawn balance.
Some 'hard core' overdrafts have been used to finance plant and machinery. However it is generally regarded as more prudent for longer-term assets to be financed by longer-term funds, rather than by overdrafts which have a variable rate of interest and which are technically repayable on demand. The result has been the growth of term lending in the past few years. About half the banks' lending now takes the form of term loans repayable over periods ranging from a year to as much as twenty years. These loans can be tailored to the circumstances of the borrowers, term loans are particularly suitable for financing investments in new assets where the repayment schedule can be related to the cash flow, they have an increasing relevance for firms with plans for expansion.

Special term lending schemes

1. Term loans include both conventional medium term loans and term lending schemes designed specifically for the small firm. An important feature of some of these schemes is the option to repay at a fixed rather than variable rate of interest. Even where the rate is variable, the actual monthly repayments remain unchanged, with movements in rates being accommodated in the length of the repayment period. These loans schemes have proved extremely popular with small firms. The following chart illustrates the main term lending schemes available, at the time of writing.

2. **Barclays** introduced its Business Expansion Loans in 1980. Loans are available up to twenty year terms and are designed to assist small and medium sized firms in the financing of capital expenditure projects. Between £5,000 and £500,000 is offered through branches, larger sums may be borrowed through Barclays Merchant Bank. Fixed and variable rate loans are available and the only security required is the assets purchased. Barclays also launched its Business Start Loan scheme in 1980. Loans are primarily to provide finance for new companies to launch new projects or products. Loans between £5,000 and £100,000 are available for up to five years to cover expenditure on fixed assets, research and development costs, and anticipated losses in the first two years. There are two unusual features, first, no repayment of capital is required until the end of the term, second, instead of interest, the borrowing company pays a royalty to the bank, linked to the level of its sales. In March, 1983, Barclays introduced a

Table 1
The banks' main term lending schemes

	Upper Limit (£)	Fixed or Variable Rate	Maximum Term (years)
Barclays			
Business Expansion Loans	500,000	Both	20
Business Start Loans	100,000	No interest as such; royalty linked to sales	5
Lloyds			
Asset Loans	25,000	Fixed	5
Enterprise Loans	250,000	Variable	10
Midland			
Medium-term Loans	No Maximum	Both	10
Long-term Loans	500,000	Both	20
National Westminster			
Business Development Loans	250,000	Fixed	20
Williams & Glyn's			
Business Borrowing Plan	250,000	Variable	10
	100,000	Both	5
Bank of Scotland	No Maximum	Both	20
Royal Bank of Scotland			
Business Term Loan	No Maximum	Both	20
Clydesdale			
Medium-term Loans	No Maximum	Variable	10

further term lending facility, the Basis Loan scheme. Loans are provided by Barclays Development Capital for up to ten years. The scheme is designed for firms whose borrowing needs cannot be fully accommodated by straightforward loan finance. In addition to the loan Barclays Development Capital takes an equity stake in the firm.

3. **Lloyds** introduced its Asset Loans scheme to finance up to 100 per cent of the cost of premises or other capital expenditure in 1979. Loans of between £5,000 and £25,000 are available. Also Enterprise Loans from £25,000 to £250,000 were introduced for larger propositions. Both types of loans are normally secured, long-term loans for sums in excess of £250,000 are available at variable rates of interest, usually linked to money market rates.
4. Medium-term loans for small firms are available from **Midland** at fixed and variable rates for terms up to ten years. In 1980 Midland launched Venture Loans, specifically for the independent business, loans of beween £5,000 and £250,000 are available for up to ten years. Long-term loans of between £20,000 and £500,000 for periods between ten and twenty years were added to Midland's range of facilities in 1979. In some circumstances these loans give the bank the option to subscribe to a small proportion of equity.
5. **National Westminster**'s Business Development Loans were introduced in 1971. These loans at a fixed rate of interest give the benefit of fixed repayments. The maximum loan now stands at £250,000 with repayment up to twenty years.
6. **Williams and Glyn**'s Business Borrowing Plan was launched in 1980, loans of up to £250,000 are available for up to ten years. Loans in excess of £100,000 may be repaid over ten years at variable rates.
7. **The Royal Bank of Scotland**'s Business Loan scheme is up to five years at a fixed rate of interest. In addition, the Royal Bank's subsidiary, National Commercial and Glyn's provides development finance. Loans are available for up to ten years and in some cases equity participation is taken.
8. **The Bank of Scotland** does have term lending facilities for industry, small firms are the main users of these facilities.
9. **Clydesdale** — loans are available on a variable-rate basis for up to ten years.

At all the banks contact should be made initially with the local bank manager. However enquiries can also be made to the following.

Clearing banks and other domestic deposit banks

Allied Irish Banks Ltd., Area General Manager, Britain, 64/66, Coleman Street, LONDON, EC2R 5AI. 01-588-0691

Bank of Ireland, General Manager, Britain, 36, Moorgate, LONDON, EC2R 6DP. 01-628-8811/9

Bank of Scotland, The Mound, Edinburgh, EH1 1YZ. 031-229-2555

Barclays Bank Ltd., Corporate Business Department, Juxon House, St. Pauls, LONDON EC4M 8EH. 01-248 9155

Clydesdale Bank Ltd., (a member of the Midland Bank Group), Business Development Department or Export Finance Department, 30 St. Vincent Place, GLASGOW G1 2HL. 041-248 7070

Co-operative Bank Limited, Corporate Business Manager, 1, Balloon Street, MANCHESTER M60 4EP. 061-832 3456

Coutts & Co., (a member of the National Westminster Group), Head of Banking Division, 440 Strand, LONDON WC2R 0QS. 01-379 6262

Lloyds Bank Ltd., Head Office, P.O. Box 215, 71, Lombard Street, LONDON EC3P 3BS. 01-626 1500

Midland Bank Ltd., (1) Independent Business Banking Unit, Corporate Finance Division, 27/32 Poultry, LONDON EC2P 2BX. 01-606 9911

Midland Bank Ltd., (2) International Division, Corporate Finance Dept. or Export Finance Dept. 60, Gracechurch Street, LONDON EC3P 3BN. 01-606 9944

National Westminster Bank Ltd., Corporate Finance Services Section, Domestic Banking Division, 41 Lothbury, London, EC2P 2BP. 01-606 6060

Northern Bank Ltd., (a member of the Midland Bank Group), P.O. Box 183, Donegall Square West, Belfast, BT1 6JS. 0232 45277

The Royal Bank of Scotland Ltd., Business Development Manager, P.O. Box 31, 42, St. Andrew Square, Edinburgh EH2 2YE. 031-556 8555

Ulster Bank Ltd., (a member of the National Westminster Bank Group), 47, Donegall Place, Belfast, BT1 5AU. 0232 220222

Williams & Glyn's Bank Ltd., (a member of the Royal Bank of Scotland Group), 67, Lombard Street, London, EC3P 3D1. 01-623 4356

Yorkshire Bank Ltd., Controller (Marketing), 20, Merrion Way, Leeds, LS2 8NZ. 0532 441244

Central Trustee Savings Bank Ltd., Corporate Lending Department, P.O. Box 99, St. Mary's Court, 100, Lower Thames Street, LONDON, EC3R 6AQ. 01-623 5266

Advisory services

Financial advice to small businesses has always been a central element in the job of a bank manager. As the financial environment in which small firms operate has become increasingly complex, the clearing banks have recognised the need to improve the range of their advisory services. Two banks — Barclays and Lloyds — have responded by establishing business advisory services. The other banks have placed their emphasis on developing the advisory role of their branch and area managers.

Barclays set up its advisory service in response to the 1971 Bolton Report on small firms, and it started in 1973. Lloyds set up its similar service in 1976. The service is free to the bank's own customers. The main purpose is to help firms to improve their financial planning and reporting procedures — areas in which many firms are weak. Guidance is given on budgeting, forecasting, management reporting, costing, pricing, control of debtors and stocks and business systems.

Hire purchase and leasing

In both cases, the equipment being financed is hired out to the user, rather than bought outright, and in both cases the regular rental payments are fixed at the outset of the contract. The main difference is that under a hire purchase agreement, ownership of the asset eventually passes to the user, a leased asset remains the property of the lessor (hirer). Often the contract allows the lessee to pay a reduced rent after the end of an agreed period.

Leasing can be particularly appropriate for small firms whose tax situation is such that they cannot benefit from the capital allowances available on the assets being financed. The capital allowance is enjoyed instead by the lessor, who can effectively pass it on to the lessee in the form of reduced rentals.

Also the *rentals* will normally be fully allowable against tax.

Leasing companies

The following are members of the Equipment Leasing Association:

Airlease International Management Ltd., 24–28, St Mary Axe, London, EC3A 8DE. 01-626 9393

Allied Irish Finance Company Ltd., 10–12, Neeld Parade, Wembley Hill Road, Wembley, HA9 6QU. 01-903 1383

American Express Equipment Finance (UK) Ltd., 120, Moorgate, London, EC2P 2JY. 01-588 6480

Anglo Leasing Ltd., 2, Clerkenwell Green, London, EC1R 0DH. 01-234 4300

Arbuthnot Leasing International Ltd., 37, Queen Street, London, EC4R 1BY. 01-236 5281

BankAmerica Finance Ltd., Eldon Lodge, 196–200, King's Road, Reading, Berkshire, RG1 4NJ. 0734 55891

Barclays Mercantile Industrial Finance Ltd., (a member of the Barclays Bank Group), Elizabethan House, Great Queen Street, London, WC2B 5DX. 01-242 1234

Robert Benson Lonsdale & Co. Ltd., 20, Fenchurch Street, London, EC3P 3DB. 01-623 8000

Bowmaker Leasing Ltd., Bowmaker House, Christchurch Road, Bournemouth, BH1 3LG. 0202 22077

British Credit Trust Ltd., 34, High Street, Slough, SL1 1ED. 0753 73211

British Industrial Corporation (Leasing) Ltd., P.O. Box 243, 30, Gresham Street, London, EC2P 2EB. 01-600 4555

Capital Leasing Ltd., (a member of the Bank of Scotland Group), 4, Melville Street, Edinburgh, EH3 7NZ. 031-226 4071

Carolina Leasing Ltd., 14, Austin Friars, London, EC2N 2EH. 01-588 9133

Chartered Trust Ltd., 24–26, Newport Road, Cardiff, CF2 1SR. 0222 484484

Charterhouse Japhet Leasing Ltd., 2, The Courtyard, Denmark Street, Wokingham, Berkshire, RG11 2AZ. 0734 790202

Chase Manhattan Ltd., P.O. Box 16, Woolgate House, Coleman Street, London, EC2P 2HD. 01-638 6999

Citicorp International Bank Ltd., 355, Strand, London, WC2. 01-836 1230

City Leasing Ltd., 23, Great Winchester Street, London, EC2P 2AX. 01-588 4545

Commercial Credit Leasing Ltd., 125, High Street, Croydon, Surrey, CR9 1PU. 01-686 3466

CTSB Leasing Ltd., (a member of the Trustee Savings Banks Group), P.O. Box 99, St Mary's Court, 100, Lower Thames Street, London, EC3R 6AQ. 01-623 5266

Eastlease Ltd., 8, Surrey Street, Norwich, Norfolk, NR1 3ST. 0603 22200 ext. 2555

ELCO Leasing Ltd., 41, Bishopsgate, London, EC2P 2AA. 01-253 9911

European Banking Co. Ltd., 150, Leadenhall Street, London, EC3V 4PP. 01-638 3654

F.C. Finance Ltd., Stratford House, Station Road, Godalming, Surrey, GU7 1HH. 048 68 4141

First Dallas Ltd., 16, St Helen's Place, London, EC3A 6BY. 01-638 6171

Forward Trust Group Ltd., (a member of the Midland Bank Group), Broad Street House, 55, Old Broad Street, London. EC2M 1RX. 01-920 0141

GKN Sankey Finance Ltd., P.O. Box 31, Albert Street, Bilston, West Midlands, WV14 0DL. 0902 44456

Gray Dawes Leasing Ltd., 40, St Mary Axe, London, EC3A 8EU. 01-283 6921

Grindlays Bank Group, Leasing Department, P.O. Box 280, 23, Fenchurch Street, London, EC3P 3ED. 01-626 0545

Hambros Bank Ltd., Equipment Leasing Department, 41, Bishopsgate, London, EC2P 2AA. 01-588 2851

Hamilton Leasing Ltd., Hamilton House, 80, Stokes Croft, Bristol, BS1 3QW. 0272 48080

Highland Leasing Ltd., Elstree House, Elstree Way, Borehamwood, Herts. 01-207-4488

Hill Samuel Leasing Co. Ltd., 100, Wood Street, London, EC2P 2AJ. 01-628 8011

ICFC Leasing Ltd., 91, Waterloo Road, London, SE1 8XP. 01-928 7822

Lloyds Leasing Ltd., (a member of the Lloyds Bank Group), 57, Southwark Street, London, SE1 1SH. 01-403 1600

Lloyds and Scottish (Leasing) Ltd., Finance House, Orchard Brae, Edinburgh, EH4 1PF. 031-332 2451

Lombard and Ulster Leasing Ltd., (a member of the National Westminster Bank Group), Canada House, 22, North Street, Belfast, BT1 1JX. 0232 29261

Lombard North Central Ltd., (a member of the National Westminster Bank Group), Lombard House, Curzon Street, Park Lane, London, W1A 1EU. 01-409 3434

Lynn Regis Finance Ltd., 10, Tuesday Market Place, King's Lynn, Norfolk, PE30 1JL. 0553 3465

Nordic Leasing Ltd., Nordic Bank House, 20, St Dunstans Hill, London, EC3R 8HY. 01-621 1111

North West Securities Ltd., (a member of the Bank of Scotland Group), North West House, City Road, Chester, CH1 3AN. 0244 315351

Orient Leasing Co. Ltd., London Representative Office, 14, Curzon Street, London, W1Y 7FH. 01-499 7121/2

Orion Leasing Ltd., 1, London Wall, London, EC2Y 5JX. 01-600 6222

Premier Computers Ltd., 3, Union Court, Richmond, Surrey, TW9 1AA. 01-940 1134

Rea Brothers (Leasing) Ltd., King's House, 36–37, King Street, London, EC2V 8DR. 01-606 4033

Royal Bank Leasing Ltd., (a member of the Royal Bank of Scotland Group), P.O. Box 31, 42, St Andrew Square, Edinburgh, EH2 2YE. 031-556 8555

Roytru Leasing Ltd., 107, Cheapside, London, EC2V 6DT. 01-606 3060

St Michael Finance Ltd., Michael House, Baker Street, London, W1A 1DN. 01-935 4422

Scandinavian Leasing Ltd., 36, Leadenhall Street, London, EC3A 1BH, 01-709 0565. (From March 1982 new address: Scandinavian House, 2–6, Cannon Street, London, EC4M 6XX. 01-236 6090)

Schroder Leasing Ltd., P.O. Box 99, Harrow, Middlesex, HA1 2HP. 01-863 7711

Shawlands Securities Ltd., 8, Christchurch Road, Bournemouth, BH1 3NQ. 0202 295544

Standard Chartered Leasing Co. Ltd., 79, New Cavendish Street, London, W1M 8AJ. 01-580 0302

Tiger Leasing (UK) Ltd., 173, Sloane Street, London, SW1X 9QG. 01-235 9285

United Dominions Leasing Ltd., (a member of the Trustee Savings Banks Group), 51, Eastcheap, London, EC3P 3BU. 01-623 3020

United Leasing Ltd., 14, Welbeck Street, London, W1M 7PF. 01-935 7104

Williams & Glyn's Leasing Co. Ltd., (a member of the Royal Bank of Scotland Group), 20, Birchin Lane, London, EC3P 3DP. 01-623 4356

Yorkshire Bank Leasing Ltd., 2, Infirmary Street, Leeds, LS1 2UL. 0532 443511

The following companies, not members of the Equipment Leasing Association, are those which also provide equipment leasing.

Ansbacher Leasing Ltd., 1, Noble Street, London, EC2V 7JH. 01-606 4010

Associates Capital Corporation Ltd., Associates House, P.O. Box 200, Windsor, Berkshire, SL4 1SW. 0735 57100. Branches: Canterbury, Cheadle, West Bromwich, and West Drayton

Baring Brothers & Co., Ltd., 8, Bishopsgate, London, EC2N 4AE. 01-283 8833

BNP (Finance) Ltd., 8–13, King William Street, London, EC4P 4HS. 01-626 5678

Concord Leasing Ltd., Concord House, 61 High Street, Brentford, Middlesex, TW8 0AA. 01-568 3321

First National Credit (Leasing) Ltd., First National House, College Road, Harrow, Middlesex, HA1 1FB. 01-861 1313

GGC Leasing Ltd., W.L. Leasing Ltd., Ambassador House, Brigstock Road, Thornton Heath, Surrey, CR4 7JG. 01-684 9831
Guinness Mahon Leasing Ltd., 32, St Mary-at-Hill, London, EC3P 3AJ. 01-623 9333
Humberclyde Leasing Ltd., Coulton House, Barmby Road, Pocklington, York, YO4 2DN. 075 92 2008
Lease Management Services Ltd., Lease Management Services House, 81, High Street, Esther, KT10 9QA. 78 67711
MAIBL Leasing Ltd., 26, Throgmorton Street, London, EC2N 2AH. 01-588 0271
Noble Grossart Ltd., 48, Queen Street, Edinburgh, EH2 3NR. 031-226 7011
N M Rothschild & Son (Leasing) Ltd., P.O. Box 185, New Court, St Swithin's Lane, London, EC4P 4DU. 01-626 4356
St Margaret's Leasing Ltd., (a member of the Royal Bank of Scotland Group), The Quadrangle, Imperial Square, Cheltenham, Gloucestershire, GL50 1PZ. 0242 36141
Singer & Friedlander Leasing Ltd., 20, Cannon Street, London, EC4M 6XE. 01-248 9646
SocGen Lease Ltd., 105–108, Old Broad Street, London, EC2P 2HR. 01-628 6751
Standard Chartered Merchant Bank Ltd., Company Secretary, 33–36, Gracechurch Street, London, EC3V 0AX. 01-623 8711

Finance houses

Finance houses provide instalment credit facilities, usually for up to five years, many are subsidiaries or associates of the clearing banks.

Allied Irish Finance Co. Ltd., 10–12, Neeld Parade, Wembley Hill Road, Wembley, HA9 6QU. 01-903 1383
Associates Capital Corporation Ltd., Associates House, P.O. Box 200, Windsor, Berkshire, SL4 1SW. 0735 57100. Branches: Canterbury, Cheadle, West Bromwich, and West Drayton
AVCO Financial Services Ltd., P.O. Box 154, 66–68, St Mary's Butts, Reading, Berkshire, RG1 2PE. 0734 584241
BankAmerica Finance Ltd., Eldon Lodge, 196–200, King's Road, Reading, Berkshire, RG1 4NJ. 0734 55891
Boston Trust & Savings Ltd., Boston House, Lower Dagnall Street, St Albans, Hertfordshire, AL3 4PG. 0727 32241
Bowmaker Ltd., Bowmaker House, Christchurch Road, Bournemouth, BH1 3LG. 0202 22077
Bradwell Finance Co. Ltd., Bradwell House, 16, King Street, Newcastle, Staffordshire, ST5 1ET. 0782 617879

British Credit Trust Ltd., 34, High Street, Slough, SL1 1ED. 0753 73211
Cattle's Holdings Finance Ltd., 6, Wolfreton Drive, Springfield Way, Anlaby, Hull, HU10 7BY. 0482 659371
Chartered Trust Ltd., 24–26, Newport Road, Cardiff, CF2 1SR. 0222 484484
Charterhouse Japhet Finance Ltd., 2, The Courtyard, Denmark Street, Wokingham, Berkshire, RG11 2AZ. 0734 790202
Citibank Savings, St Martin's House, Hammersmith Grove, Hammersmith, London, W6 9HW. 01-741 4621
Commercial Credit Services Ltd., Grosvenor House, 125, High Street, Croydon, CR9 1PU. 01-686 3466
F.C. Finance Ltd., Stratford House, Station Road, Godalming, Surrey, GU7 1HH. 048 68 4141
First National Securities Ltd., First National House, College Road, Harrow, Middlesex, HA1 1FB. 01-861 1313
Forthright Finance Ltd., 114–116, St Mary Street, Cardiff, CF1 1XJ. 0222 396131
Forward Trust Group Ltd., (a member of the Midland Bank Group), Broad Street House, 55, Old Broad Street, London, EC2M 1RX. 01-920 0141
HFC Trust Ltd., Cory House, The Ring, Bracknell, Berkshire, RG12 1BL. 0344 24727
ICFC Leasing Ltd., 91, Waterloo Road, London, SE1 8XP. 01-928 7822
Industrial Funding Trust Ltd., 18, St Swithin's Lane, London, EC4N 8AH. 01-623 1090
KDB Finance Ltd., Oakvale House, Chatham Road, Sandling, Maidstone, Kent, ME14 3BQ. 0622 57294
Lloyds and Scottish Finance Ltd., Finance House, Orchard Brae, Edinburgh, EH4 1PF. 031-332 2451
Lombard and Ulster Ltd., (a member of the National Westminster Bank Group), Canada House, 22, North Street, Belfast, BT1 1JX. 0232 29261
Lombard North Central Ltd., (a member of the National Westminster Bank Group), Lombard House, Curzon Street, Park Lane, London, W1A 1EU. 01-409 3434
Lynn Regis Finance Ltd., 10, Tuesday Market Place, King's Lynn, Norfolk, PE30 1JL. 0553 3465
Medens Ltd., 46–50 Southwick Square, Southwick, Brighton, BN4 4UA. 0273 593358
Mercantile Credit Company Ltd., (a member of the Barclays Bank Group), P.O. Box 75, Elizabethan House, Great Queen Street, London, WC2B 5DP. 01-242 1234.

M. H. Credit Corporation Ltd., Director and General Manager, 50, East Street, Epsom, Surrey, KT17 1HQ. 78 41407
Milford Mutual Facilities Ltd., Milford House, 29, Ardwick Green North, Manchester, M12 6HB. 061-273 2531
North British Securities Ltd., c/o P.O. Box 82, Paragon House, Ferensway, Hull, HU1 3BL. 0482 23815
North West Securities Ltd., (a member of the Bank of Scotland Group), North West House, City Road, Chester, CH1 3AN. 0244 31531
St Margaret's Trust Ltd., (a member of the Royal Bank of Scotland Group), The Quadrangle, Imperial Square, Cheltenham, GL50 1PZ. 0242 36141
Security Pacific Finance Ltd., 72 Berkeley Avenue, Reading, Berkshire. RG1 6PL. 0734 54881
Service Finance Corporation Ltd., Winston Hall, East Park Road, Blackburn, Lancashire, BB1 8BD. 0254 56521/
Shawlands Securities Ltd., 8, Christchurch Road, Bournemouth, BH1 3NQ. 0202 295544
United Dominions Trust Ltd., (a member of the Trustee Savings Banks Group), 51, Eastcheap, London, EC3P 3BU. 01-623 3020
Vernons Finance Corporation, Vernons Building, Mile End, Liverpool, L5 5AF. 051-207 3181
Wagon Finance Ltd., 3, Endcliffe Crescent, Sheffield, S10 3EE. 0742 664466
Wrenwood Finance Co. Ltd., Cleveland House, Victoria Road, Hartlepool, TS24 7SD. 0429 72245/6
Yorkshire Bank Finance Ltd., 2, Infirmary Street, Leeds, LS1 2UL. 0532 442511

Factoring

Again your approach should be to the bank as most of the clearing banks have subsidiary or associate companies which specialise in factoring. This is a service based on a book-keeping function but can also mean the provision of finance. There are four main components to factoring:
(i) The administration of the sales ledger; the responsibility for dispatching invoices and ensuring they are paid.
(ii) credit information: the factoring company can provide accurate credit ratings on firms.
(iii) the factoring company guarantees payment on approved sales.
(iv) Finance: the customer may receive up to 80% of the value of invoices as soon as they are dispatched. Factoring often results in the speedier settlement of trade debts.

Factoring Companies

Alex Lawrie Factors Ltd, Beaumont House, Beaumont Road, Banbury, Oxfordshire, OX16 7RN. 0295 4491. Branches: Bristol, Coventry, Edinburgh, London, Manchester, Newcastle, and Stockport.
Arbuthnot Factors Ltd., Arbuthnot House, Breeds Place, Hastings, Sussex, TN34 3DG. 0424 430824
Barclays Factoring Ltd., (a member of the Barclays Bank Group), P.O. Box 9, Paddington House, Basingstoke, RG21 1BE. 0256 56161
Credit Factoring International Ltd., (a member of the National Westminster Bank Group), Smith House, P.O. Box 50, Elmwood Avenue, Feltham, Middlesex, TW13 7QD. 01-890 1390
Forward Trust Group Ltd., (a member of the Midland Bank Group), Griffin House, 21, Farncombe Road, Worthing, Sussex, BN11 2BW. 0903 205181
H and H Factors Ltd., Randolph House, 46–48 Wellesley Road, Croydon, Surrey, CR9 3PS 01-681 2641
Independent Factors Ltd., International Factors Ltd., Sovereign House, 98–99, Queen's Road, Brighton, BN1 3WZ. 0273 21211

Export finance

The clearing banks play a major role in helping firms finance their export sales. The services include facilities for drawing upon documentary credits established by the importer's bankers, as well as financing of the exports themselves, through advances or by discounting the bills that the exporter draws on shipment. The banks also provide advice on the services available from the Export Credits Guarantee Department.
Financial arrangements for exporting differ from domestic business. Anyone planning to export should first seek advice from his bank on obtaining the finance that may be needed. Finance can be made available to cover the whole cycle of production, shipment and payment by the overseas buyer.
Export finance from a bank may be made on bills of exchange drawn under an export contract. Alternatively bills can be sold outright to a bank or discount house to provide short-term finance.

ECGD — supported finance

The Government do not themselves provide export finance; however, exporters who insure the credit they give their overseas buyers with the Export Credits Guarantee Department (ECGD) will normally be in a more favourable position to obtain finance from a bank.

ECGD credit insurance

The basic ECGD policy is a comprehensive short-term guarantee and provides cover against the main risks of non-payment. This could arise from the insolvency or default of the buyer or from 'political' causes. ECGD expects an exporter holding this policy to offer for cover all his exports which are sold on terms of payment of 180 days or less; for this he pays a monthly premium. Exporters apply limits to the insured credit. Once a credit limit has been granted, it is revolving: as payments are received an exporter can grant further credit up to the set limit.

Post-shipment finance may be obtained from banks under a normal overdraft facility and, in connection with this, ECGD credit insurance is generally accepted as collateral. Exporters may assign an ECGD credit insurance policy to their bank.

ECGD bank guarantees

An exporter holding an ECGD policy may be able to supplement his policy with an ECGD guarantee. With this guarantee, the banks provide finance from the date of shipment at the favourable interest rate of $\frac{5}{8}$% over bank base rates.

As well as contacting your local bank it's also worth writing to the
British Export Houses Association,
69 Canon Street,
LONDON EC4N 5AB
who will provide details on exporting.

Equity finance (venture capital)

The equity capital of a business is the owners' capital permanently invested, together with any undistributed profits. Most businesses begin with an individual providing equity capital from his own resources.

In recent years the banks have become more directly involved in equity financing by launching special schemes to help meet the equity needs of their small business customers. These investments are generally through subsidiary companies.

In addition to providing venture capital to the new enterprise and development capital to the established, expanding enterprise, the banks may also acquire shares. The banks can help to ensure that control of a family firm remains within the family, by providing a mixture of loan and equity finance. The following section is a guide to development and venture capital facilities.

Vehicle for capital	*Backers*	*Type of client or situation*	*Min/Max funds injected*	*Start up capital*	*Equity stake*	*Term of funding*
Abingworth *Tel: (01) 839 6745*	Leading UK and European institutions	Usually established profitable companies	£100,000-£500,000 and occasionally larger amounts	Possibly, if management of proven calibre	Always minority	Open
Advent Eurofund Ltd *Tel: Jersey (0534) 75151*	Monsanto—50% UK financial institutions universities and colleges —50%	New technology at all stages of development	£100,000 to £500,000	Yes, but not exclusively	Significant minority	Flexible
Anglo-American Venture Fund Ltd *Tel: (061) 236 7302*	British Technology Group (BTG)	New technology, with emphasis on electronics	Up to £300,000 but will syndicate	Yes	Yes	Equity and preference shares
APA Venture Capital Fund *Tel: (01) 388 1811*	Pension funds, Insurance companies and institutions primarily from the UK	Companies with high growth prospects, management buy-outs	£100,000-£1m.	Yes	Minority equity investments	Approximately 5 years

Vehicle for capital	Backers	Type of client or situation	Min/Max funds injected	Start up capital	Equity stake	Term of funding
Barclays Development Capital *Tel: (01) 623 4321*	Barclays Bank Group	Established growth companies earning £100,000 + pre-tax	£150,000 minimum but may sindicate large investments	No	Yes, 10–40%	Open
Biotechnology Investments Limited *Tel: (01) 280 5000*	NM Rothschild and leading UK institutions	Biotechnology companies worldwide at all stages of development	Flexible: generally $500,000–$2m; would syndicate larger investments	Yes	Up to 20%, exceptionally higher	Flexible; usually equity
Birmingham Technology Ltd *Tel: Birmingham (021) 359 0981*	Lloyds Bank PLC; Birmingham City Council; University of Aston in Birmingham	Hi-tech research, development and/or hi-tech manufacturing companies	Depending on requirements	Yes	Possibly, but not exclusively	Flexible according to requirements

Vehicle for capital	*Backers*	*Type of client or situation*	*Min/Max funds injected*	*Start up capital*	*Equity stake*	*Term of funding*
British Technology Group (BTG) *Tel: (01) 403 6666*	HM Government	Companies of all sizes, engaged in advanced technology. Two special schemes for small companies. Regional finance available	As appropriate	Yes	Yes	Finance provided in form of share capital or project finance. Equity, preference and loan capital offered on venture capital terms
Brown Shipley Developments *Tel: (01) 606 9833*	Brown, Shipley & Co.	Quality of individuals of prime importance and above average growth sectors	£50,000 minimum equity preferance shares, may syndicate larger investments and loans	Yes, if individuals have previous experience	Yes, usuall 10–30%	Equity: open Loans: up to 8 years
Candover Investments *Tel: (01) 583 5090*	7 leading UK institutions	Management buy-outs and conventional development capital situations	£2m +	No	Always minority	Open

Vehicle for capital	*Backers*	*Type of client or situation*	*Min/Max funds injected*	*Start up capital*	*Equity stake*	*Term of funding*
Capital Partners International *Tel: (01) 351 4899*	Private European Investors	Companies with overseas expansion potential, i.e. an internationally marketable know-how	£10,000-£350,000 Would form syndicate for larger investments	Yes, if management has relevant experience, a detailed business plan and exceptional growth potential	Yes	Flexible to suit each situation
Capital Ventures Ltd *Tel: Glos (0242) 584380*	The Colgrave Fund supported by private investors	New or recently established business ventures qualifying for inclusion under the 1981 Business Start-Up	£25,000–£600,000. ordinary capital. Complete package with loan/preference gearing can be arranged	Yes	Yes, 10–49%	Equity to be held for a minimum of 5 years
Castle Finance *Tel: Norwich (0603) 22200*	Norwich Union insurance	Profitable private companies requiring capital for expansion	Normally £30,000–£500,000	Exceptionally	Yes, up to 30%	Medium and long term loans — fixed or viable interest

Vehicle for capital	*Backers*	*Type of client or situation*	*Min/Max funds injected*	*Start up capital*	*Equity stake*	*Term of funding*
Cayzer, Gartmore Investments Limited *Tel: (01) 623 1212*	Cayzer Gartmore, subsidiary of British & Commonwealth Shipping	Small and medium sized companies with growth potential requiring equity and/or loan capital	£0.2m–2m Larger sums syndicated	Exceptionally	Yes. Minority	Medium
Charterhouse Development *Tel: (01) 606 7070*	Charterhouse Group	Companies of above average quality, i.e. with good growing earnings	£250,000	No	Yes	Open
CIN Industrial Finance *Tel: (01) 353 1500*	National Coal Board Pension Funds	Small and medium sized companies public or private with growth potential Equity subscription loan and equity packages, development capital and project finance are undertaken	£500,000–£2m — smaller amounts are referred to our small companies investment	Yes, this is also referred to our small companies investment fund fund	Yes, 10–49%	Medium and long term loans available only with some form of equity participation

Vehicle for capital	*Backers*	*Type of client or situation*	*Min/Max funds injected*	*Start up capital*	*Equity stake*	*Term of funding*
Citicorp Development Capital *Tel: (01) 438 1280*	Citicorp/ Citibank	Expansion capital for technology growth companies. Management buy-outs Acquisition etc, finance for mature companies	£200,000–£5m	Exceptionally; proven management team and high growth prospects required	Yes 10–40% desired	Open Structured to suit company requirement
Clydesdale Bank Industrial Finance *Tel: Glasgow (041) 248 7070*	Clydesdale Bank/ Midland Bank	Profitable private companies with potential for growth	Normally £100,000 + but will consider proposals at lower level	Yes — highly selective	Normally 20–40%	Open
Commercial Bank of the Near East *Tel: (01) 283 4041*	Range of shareholders predominant Greek	Small and medium sized companies public & private	Up to £400,000	Yes	No	Open

Vehicle for capital	*Backers*	*Type of client or situation*	*Min/Max funds injected*	*Start up capital*	*Equity stake*	*Term of funding*
Commonwealth Development Finance Company Ltd *Tel: (01) 407 9711*	Several Commonwealth Central Banks and 140 major UK companies	Company with proven management and profit record preferably seeking funds for expansion	£300,000 to £1.5m	No	Yes, 10–45%	Up to ten years
Council for Small Industries in Rural Areas (CoSIRA) *Tel: Salisbury (0722) 6255*	HM Government plus financial institutions Including ICF under new scheme	Companies with no more than 20 skilled employees in countryside or in towns with less than 10,000 population	£250–£75,000 or maximum $\frac{1}{3}$ or $\frac{1}{2}$ of project cost, depending upon location	Loans are available for new starters	No	Building loans — 20 yrs. Working capital — Equipment loans — 5 yrs.
County Bank *Tel: (01) 638 6000*	National Westminster Bank	Any growing company with proven management; finance for the company, to enable shareholders to realise part of their investment or to assist management in buying an equity stake	£100,000 +	Yes for sound projects	If appropriate often 10–15% usually less than 25%	Loans up to 20 years; equity open

Vehicle for capital	*Backers*	*Type of client or situation*	*Min/Max funds injected*	*Start up capital*	*Equity stake*	*Term of funding*
Development Capital Group *Tel: (01) 486 5021*	Insurance & Pension funds, industrial companies and a major clearing bank	Proven management. Minimum £100,000 pretax profit potential	£150,000-£1.5m +	Yes, under certain circumstances	Yes, minority	5 years upwards
East of Scotland Industrial Investments *Tel: Edinburgh (031) 225 7515*	Leading UK Institutions	Established profitable companies	£20,000-£400,000	Occasionally, if proven management	Always minority	Equity and long term loan capital
East of Scotland Onshore *Tel: Edinburgh (031) 225 7515*	Leading UK institutions	Established companies — the oil service sector	£30,000–£1m	Occasionally if provem management	Yes, always minority	Equity and long term capital
EDITH PLC *Tel: (01) 928 7822*	Listed authorised investment trust, (managed by ICFC)	Established private and unlisted public companies and smaller listed companies	£5,000–£1m	No	Yes, minority, enabling shareholders to realise investment	Provision of cash or exchange of shares for personal shareholders of family trusts

Vehicle for capital	*Backers*	*Type of client or situation*	*Min/Max funds injected*	*Start up capital*	*Equity stake*	*Term of funding*
Electra Risk Capital *Tel: (01) 836 7766*	Private individual investors	Investment qualifying for business start up relief. Start-ups and companies who have traded for less than five years	£100,000 to £750,000 over a period	Yes	Yes to 50%	Only equity investment — no dividend
English & Caledonian PLC *Tel: (01) 626 7197 (01) 283 3531*	Clients of Gartmore Investment, Scottish United Investors and other investors	Private companies able and willing to obtain a USM placing or a full listing within 5 years	£200,000–£750,000. Larger sums can be syndicated among existing shareholders	Yes, if management has previous experience in similar markets	Yes 10–49%	Preferably an equity stake. Loans can be arranged subject to an equity stake
Equity Capital for Industry *Tel: (01) 606 8513*	City Industrial institutions	£200,000–£2m companies with capitalisation of £1m–£40m or similar unquoted	Exceptionally smaller sums available from associate fund	Yes, usually	Long term: 5–25%	equity/ convertible/ loan package tailored to circumstances

Vehicle for capital	*Backers*	*Type of client or situation*	*Min/Max funds injected*	*Start up capital*	*Equity stake*	*Term of funding*
European Investment Bank (European Community's long term bank) *Tel: (01) 222 2933*	1) Scheme operated by DoI and Scottish, Welsh and Northern Ireland Offices 2) Schemes operated by ICFC, Midland Bank 3) Schemes operated by WDA, SDA and Clydesdale Bank 4) Scheme operated by ICFC (under Orto facility)	For small and medium sized ventures (in UK assisted areas for 1, 2 + 3)	In all cases maximum contribution is 50% of fixed asset cost of project 1) Loans between 15,000 and £4.25m 2) £15,000 and £2m 3) £15,000 and £250,000 4) £15,000–£250,000	Loans can be made for sound projects by new companies with adequate equity	No	1) 7 years including 2 year capital repayment moratorium. Fixed rate in region of 9% 2, 3 + 4) Up to 8 years including 2 year capital repayment moratorium. Fixed rate in region of 10% region of 11%
Federation Pension Fund *Tel: (01) 636 3828*	The National Federation of Self Employed and Small Businesses, City of Westminster Assurance	Established self employed/small business; 3 year record; must be a member of the Federation	£15,000-£250,000 now under review	No	No	Up to 20 years

Vehicle for capital	*Backers*	*Type of client or situation*	*Min/Max funds injected*	*Start up capital*	*Equity stake*	*Term of funding*
First Welsh General Investment Trust Limited *Tel: Cardiff (0222) 396131*	Commercial Bank of Wales PLC	Management buy-out	Subject to negotiation	In certain circumstances	Yes and/or option — not essential	Up to ten years
Fountain Development Capital Fund *Tel: (01) 628 8011*	Hill Samuel, pension funds and insurance companies	Any company with two years trading record	£50,000–£750,000	Yes in certain situations	Always minority	Equity and/or loan
Greater London Enterprise Board *Tel: (01) 633 1487*	Greater London Council	Must be of 'benefit to London'	Up to £1m but higher in exceptional circumstances	Yes	As necessary	—
Gresham Trust *Tel: (01) 606 6474*	Grovewood Securities Ltd (Ultimate holding company Eagle Star Holdings PLC)	Profitable private companies looking for expansion realisation of shareholder's interests, help in management buy-outs	£50,000-£500,000 Will syndicate larger amounts	Where experience and track record exists in previous business	Usually, but always a minority holding	Preference shares or loans: 5–10 Equity: Open

Vehicle for capital	*Backers*	*Type of client or situation*	*Min/Max funds injected*	*Start up capital*	*Equity stake*	*Term of funding*
Guldehouse Limited *Tel: (01) 606 6321*	Private	Completely open and flexible Syndicated purchases, management buy-outs, USM venture or development capital	Up to £200,000 directly—syndicate or advise in larger situations	Yes	Preferably yes, but flexible approach, e.g. royalty income	Open and flexible
Hafren Investment Finance Ltd. *Tel: Treforest (044 385) 2666*	Welsh Development Agency	High growth operations	£10,000–£100,000	Yes	Yes	Open
Hambro International Venture Fund	Various	Growth Companies	\$250,000–\$500,000	Yes	Yes	Variable
Hambros Advanced Technology Trust	Hambros Bank	Technology Industries High Growth	£100,000–£500,000	Yes	Yes	5 yrs typical

Vehicle for capital	*Backers*	*Type of client or situation*	*Min/Max funds injected*	*Start up capital*	*Equity stake*	*Term of funding*
Highlands and Islands Development Board *Tel: Inverness (0463) 34171*	HM Government (Scottish Office)	Manufacturing, tourist, agriculture, fisheries and other industries in the Scottish Highlands and Islands	Up to £400,000	Yes	Up to 40%	5–10 years. 20 years for building loans
Industrial and Commercial Finance Corporation (ICFC) *Tel: (01) 928 7822*	Finance for Industry (Bank of England and clearing banks)	Small and medium sized companies public and private	£5,000–£2m	Yes	Yes, minority	Fixed interest loans medium and long term
Innotech Investments Limited *Tel: (01) 834 2492*	Private Individuals	Fast growing small to medium sized companies operating in higher technology areas	£100,000 to £500,000	Exceptionally	Yes — minority (25 to 40%)	Equity: open Loans: 3–6 years

Vehicle for capital	*Backers*	*Type of client or situation*	*Min/Max funds injected*	*Start up capital*	*Equity stake*	*Term of funding*
INTEX Executives (UK) Ltd + E.P. Woods Investments Ltd. *Tel: (01) 831 6925/ 242-2263*	Private and institutional investors and trusts	Industrial and commercial enterprises, with special reference to high technology and innovation	\$10,000 to \$1m	Yes	Usually minority only. In appropriate circumstances up to 75%	Equity and loan arranged according to circumstances
Larpent Newton & Co Ltd *Tel: (01) 831 9991*	Advisory work for leading UK institutions	Unquoted companies requiring development capital and management buy-outs	£50,000–£2m	Yes with experienced management	Usually	Individually tailored
LEDU — The small Business Agency for Northern Ireland *Tel: (0232) 691031*	Department of Economic Development	Mainly manufacturing and service companies employing up to 50 people in Northern Ireland	£1,500 +	Loans, guarantees and grants available	Yes	Grants/ loans/ guarantees average 5 years

Vehicle for capital	*Backers*	*Type of client or situation*	*Min/Max funds injected*	*Start up capital*	*Equity stake*	*Term of funding*
Leopold Joseph & Sons Ltd *Tel: (01) 588 2323*	Leopold Joseph & Sons Ltd and clients	Good management track record, companies with growth record pretax profit in excess of £100,000	Open	Exceptionally where entreprenuers have previous experience and can make a sound financial contribution	Yes	Open
Lovat Enterprise Fund *Tel: (01) 621 1212*	NCB Pension Funds, Legal & General Prudential, Electra Investment Trust, Equitable Life	Expansion financing, mainly private companies earning £100,000 + pre-tax	£100,000–£1m	No	5–40%	Open
Mathercourt Securities Limited *Tel: (01) 831 9001*	Private & institutional investors	Private UK companies including USM candidates. Close working relationship with management	£25,000–£3.5m syndicates as appropriate	Yes	Yes, 3–30%	Tailored to suit circum-stances

Vehicle for capital	*Backers*	*Type of client or situation*	*Min/Max funds injected*	*Start up capital*	*Equity stake*	*Term of funding*
Melville Street Investments *Tel: Edinburgh (031) 226 4071*	The British Linen Bank, The Airways Pension Scheme, The Standard Life Assurance Company, Scottish American Investment Company, Scottish Northern Investment Trust, The Edinburgh Investment Trust	Profitable companies with good financial discipline and new companies with established management	£50,000–£500,000 May syndicate larger investments	Yes	Minority	Long term capital
Meritor Investments *Tel: (01) 606 2179*	Midland Bank, Rolls Royce Pension Fund	Development situations and shareholders' needs	£100,000–£250,000 May syndicate larger investments	No	Yes, minority	Open
Merseyside Enterprise Fund Ltd *Tel: (051) 227 1366*	British Technology Group (BTG)	Start ups and small companies with growth potential	Up to £100,000– syndicate larger investments	Yes	Yes	Open

Vehicle for capital	*Backers*	*Type of client or situation*	*Min/Max funds injected*	*Start up capital*	*Equity stake*	*Term of funding*
Midland Bank Industrial Equity Holdings Group *Tel: (01) 638 8861*	Midland Bank	Development situations and shareholders needs	£5,000–£2m	Yes	Yes, minority	Open
Minster Trust *Tel: (01) 623 1050*	Minster Assets	Small and medium sized companies, public and private companies looking for expansion realisation of shareholders' interests, help for management for buying equity	£100,000–£250,000	Exceptionally, where entrepreneurs have previous experience	Yes minority	Open
Montagu Investment Management Limited *Tel: (01) 588 1750*	Quoted Investment Trusts	Small and medium sized companies public or private, with growth otential	Normally £200,000 to £3m	Only occasionally	Yes minority	Open

Vehicle for capital	*Backers*	*Type of client or situation*	*Min/Max funds injected*	*Start up capital*	*Equity stake*	*Term of funding*
Moracrest Investments *Tel: (01) 628 8409*	Midland Bank, Prudential Group and British Gas Pension Fund	Development situations and shareholders' needs	£200,000 + May syndicate larger investments	Yes	Yes, minority	Open
National Westminster Bank under the terms of Capital Loan Scheme (Approach through local Branch but if guidance is needed to identify a suitable branch) *Tel: (01) 726 1891*		Companies engaged in or planning to set up a business with good growth prospects backed by sound management; must bank or be willing to bank with National Westminster Bank	£10,000-£100,000	Yes	An option to subscribe for shares is taken by a subsidiary, Growth Options Limited, usually for less than 25% always for less than 50%	Up to 10 years
Newmarket Co. (1981) Ltd. (U.K. subsidiary Newmarket (Venture (Capital) Ltd.) *Tel: (01) 638 4551*	London listed company with institutional and general public shareholders	Application of new technology or innovation	Normally U.S. $200,000–$1m but occasionally higher	Yes, but not exclusively	Never a controlling stake	Primarily equity; no requirement for immediate income

Vehicle for capital	*Backers*	*Type of client or situation*	*Min/Max funds injected*	*Start up capital*	*Equity stake*	*Term of funding*
Noble Grossart investments *Tel: Edinburgh (031) 226 7011*	Noble Grossart and Scottish institutional shareholders	Good management in growth "buy-out" or turnround situations	£50,000–£1m	Yes, if the management has good track record in previous business	Yes, usually 20–40%	Open
Northern Venture Capital Syndicate *Tel: (031) 557 3560*	Private individuals under the Business Start-Up Scheme	Investments qualifying for Business Start-up Scheme i.e. start-ups and companies trading for less than 5 years	£25,000 to £75,000	Yes	Yes — up to 50%	Equity capital. Dividends not a priority
Oakland Management Holdings Limited *Tel: Hungerford Berks (04886) 3555*	A leading UK institution	New technology growth opportunities	£50,000–£250,000	Not normally	Yes	Flexible up to 7 years

Vehicle for capital	*Backers*	*Type of client or situation*	*Min/Max funds injected*	*Start up capital*	*Equity stake*	*Term of funding*
Oakwood Loan Finance Ltd *Tel: (01) 403 6666*	British Technology Group (BTG)	Small companies with growth potential	£15,000–£50,000	Yes	10% to 20% by option	Option linked, unsecured, 5-year loan. 3-year capital repayment holiday
PA Developments Ltd *Tel: (01) 589 7050*	Merchant Navy Officers' Pension Fund	Profitable private companies requiring capital for expansion or purchase of existing equity packages stakes. Particularly service industries or technology-based companies	£200,000– to £1m	No	Yes, up to 40%	Equity preferably but will consider equity/loan

Vehicle for capital	*Backers*	*Type of client or situation*	*Min/Max funds injected*	*Start up capital*	*Equity stake*	*Term of funding*
Pegasus Holdings Limited *Tel: (01) 626 1500*	Lloyds Bank Group	Management buy-out, development capital, replacement capital. For companies with proven management, pre-tax profits in excess of £50,000, and with growth potential	Minimum £100,00. No maximum, but may syndicate large investments	No	Yes. Usually 10–33⅓%	Flexible
Prudential Assurance Company Ltd *Tel: (01) 405 9222*	Prudential Group	Primarily development capital situations and buy-outs	Typically £50,000–£1m	Occasionally	Yes	Open
Prutec *Tel: (01) 828 2082*	Member of the Prudential Group	Development of high technology	Open	Yes	Up to 49%	Open

Vehicle for capital	*Backers*	*Type of client or situation*	*Min/Max funds injected*	*Start up capital*	*Equity stake*	*Term of funding*
Rainford Venture Capital *Tel: St. Helens (0744) 37227*	Pilkington Prudential, St. Helens Trust and others	Entrepreneurs; start-up or rapid growth in North West	£50,000–£350,000	Yes	Yes, but preferably not control	Primarily equity. Loans where appropriate to agreed terms
Safeguard Industrial Investments *Tel: (01) 581 4455*	Over 84% of shares held by 17 major insurance companies or pension funds	Small or medium sized UK companies	£50,000–£250,000	Exceptional	Yes	Medium to long
Scottish Allied Investors *Tel: Glasgow (041) 204 1321 (041) 226 3551*	James Finlay, Royal Bank Development Ltd, Scottish Western Trust Co. Ltd.	Profitable private companies looking for expansion capital	£50,000–£500,000	No	Yes, between 20–49%	Medium or long term investment in equity or loan/equity package
Scottish Development Agency *Tel: Glasgow (041) 248 2700* **Small Business Division** *Tel: Edinburgh (031) 343 1911*	UK Government	Manufacturing and service businesses operating in Scotland	Open	Yes	Where appropriate	2–20 years equity open

Vehicle for capital	*Backers*	*Type of client or situation*	*Min/Max funds injected*	*Start up capital*	*Equity stake*	*Term of funding*
Scottish Offshore Investors *Tel: Glasgow (041) 204 1321*	James Finlay and other financial institutions	Energy related service companies with growth prospects	£50,000–£250,00	Exceptionally	Yes, between 20–49%	Medium or long term. Equity or loan/equity
Second Northern Venture Capital Syndicate *Tel: (031) 557 3560*	Private individuals under the Business Start-Up Scheme	Investment qualifying for Business Start-Up Scheme i.e. start-ups and companies trading for less than 5 years	£25,000 min.	Yes	Yes — up to 50%	Equity capital dividends not a priority
Sharp Unquoted Midland Investment *Tel: Birmingham (021) 236 5801*	Legal & General, Royal Insurance Sun Life Assurance Society and others	Successful private companies and management buy-outs	£150,000–£850,000	No	10–35%	Open
Small Company Innovation Fund (SCIF) *Tel: (01) 403 6666*	British Technology Group (BTG)	Small companies involved in technological and innovative activities	£15,000 to £60,000	Yes	Yes, 10% to 35%	Equity plus preference shares and unsecured loan

Vehicle for capital	*Backers*	*Type of client or situation*	*Min/Max funds injected*	*Start up capital*	*Equity stake*	*Term of funding*
Smithdown Investments *Tel: (01) 408 1502*	Private individuals	Start-up situations and very small companies	£5,000–50,000	Yes	Normally	Open
Stewart Fund Managers *Tel: Edinburgh (031) 226 3271*	Scottish American Investment, Stewart Enterprise investment	Fast growing companies	£50,000-£500,000	Exceptionally only	Yes, but always minority and can be part of a package	Open
Thamesdale Investment & Finance Co Ltd *Tel: (01) 629 8322*	American and European investors	Small/medium sized companies. Equity and loan facilities	£25,000 upwards	Yes, in exceptional circumstances	Yes, 10–40%	Open
Thomson Clive Growth Companies Fund Thomson Clive Investments *Tel: (01) 491 4809*	Leading UK institutions	Private companies requiring capital for expansion and having high quality management	£20,000–£300,000	Exceptionally if management of high quality and operations within specific areas of interest	Yes, usually minority	Open

Vehicle for capital	*Backers*	*Type of client or situation*	*Min/Max funds injected*	*Start up capital*	*Equity stake*	*Term of funding*
Trust of Property Shares PLC *Tel: (01) 486 4684*	Management support with clearing bankers	Small size private property companies with growth potential requiring capital for expansion	£25,000 to £250,000 Syndicate for larger investments with participation	Possibly, if management of proven calibre	Yes 10–35%	Open
UKP-EA Growth Fund Ltd *Tel: (01) 831 9991*	United Kingdom Provident Institution and the English Association Group PLC	Development capital situations. Management buy-outs. Not quoted companies	£50,000–£300,000 but will lead syndicates for larger sums	Only where management has successful track record in in related or similar field	Yes, usually up to 30%. Never control	A package tailored to requirement. Loans up to 10 years
Venture Founders *Tel: (0295) 65881*	British Investment Trusts	Small-medium size growth companies	£50,000–£350,000	Yes	Yes prefer minority position	Open
Welsh Development Agency *Tel: Treforest (044 385) 2666*	UK Government	Manufacturing and service industries in Wales	£2,000–£1m	Yes	Yes	15–15 years — requity open

Vehicle for capital	*Backers*	*Type of client or situation*	*Min/Max funds injected*	*Start up capital*	*Equity stake*	*Term of funding*
Western Enterprise Fund Ltd *Tel: (0803) 862271*	British Technology Group (BTG) and Dartington & Co Ltd	Start ups and small companies with growth potential	Up to £100,000 — syndicate larger investments	Yes	Yes, 10% to 49%	Open
West Midlands Enterprise Board Limited *Tel: Birmingham (021) 236 8855*	West Midlands Couny Council and various financial institutions	Manufacturing and productive service sector companies employing or likely to employ 100 + in the West Midlands	£100,000–£3m	Yes	Can provide a flexible package of loan/equity capital	Normal financial criteria, but prepared to wait for a long-term capital gain
West Yorkshire Enterprise Board Ltd *Tel: Wakefield (0924) 367111*	West Yorkshire Metropolitan County Council	Business development; plant modernisation; balance sheet reconstruction; new ventures; management buy-outs	£10,000-£500,000	Yes	Possibly	Medium/long as required

Industrial support

The following list is not exhaustive and can only give very brief details of what is available, and who will be eligible. If on reading through, you think that a particular scheme sounds relevant to you, you should contact the organisation concerned and get full details and guidelines from them. Some schemes have quite rigid application procedures and operate to specific timetables — do make sure that you are aware of any such requirements. If there is something in the literature that you do not understand, ring and ask for an explanation, the staff are usually very helpful and are quite used to dealing with such queries.

Some schemes require detailed documentation at quite an early stage and so it is essential to keep your paperwork up-to-date. When submitting applications keep a copy of the information which you have provided, so that if there are any queries about it you can refer to it quickly and give accurate answers.

The schemes do change from time to time so make sure you have the most recent version, and do keep an eye open for closing dates. With the current interest in small businesses it is to be hoped that more schemes will be set up, so watch out for announcements in the press.

The information is organised so that you can read through and pick out what grants are available to you by virtue of your location and your industry.

It is worth noting that there are a number of organisations who offer advice to small firms, both on where to seek finance and on marketing, production and a wider range of subjects of concern to the businessman. Some make a small charge for their services, while others will be prepared to offer initial advice free of charge.

Assistance by location

In considering the type of financial assistance that you may qualify for, the geographical location of your business is an important factor. A large number of the grants currently available to small businesses are dependent on where the business is sited, and you should bear this in mind when choosing your premises. Of course, you may already be committed to a particular place because of the type of business which you are starting, the location of your customers, the need to have certain specialist services on hand, or perhaps because you already have premises which you intend to operate from. Whether this is the case, or whether you are free to choose any area to start up in, you should check to see if you are eligible for any of the schemes discussed in this section.

One of the first things to establish is whether your business will be located within one of the *Assisted Areas*. The map opposite shows these areas as they are currently defined, and if you are in any doubt as to whether you come within one of them you should check with the local office of:

— Department of Industry
— Welsh Office Industry Department
— Scottish Economic Planning Department
— Northern Ireland Department of Economic Development.
  (for addresses see pages 161–62)

What are assisted areas?
In order to encourage investment in parts of the UK which have had particular problems of unemployment, the Government has designated certain parts of the country as 'areas for expansion', or Assisted Areas. Under the terms of the Industrial Development Act 1982 and the Local Employment Act 1972 there are special benefits to businesses which move to, or expand or modernise an existing operation within one of the Assisted Areas.
There are three categories of Assisted Area, and they are, in decreasing order of priority:

— Special Development Areas
— Development Areas
— Intermediate Areas

There are some grants that are available in only the first, or first and second of these categories, so again you should ensure that you know exactly what applies to you.

1. REGIONAL DEVELOPMENT GRANTS

Regional Development Grants are available towards some of the capital expenditure which is incurred in providing buildings and machinery to be used in what are known as 'qualifying activities'. The grants apply only to businesses which are located within the *Special Development and Development Areas*.

Qualifying activities
The activities referred to include most manufacturing activities, i.e. those described in Orders III–XIX of the Standard Industrial Classification, 1968.* In addition to these, the following are also included: certain repair activities, the processing of scrap and waste materials, scientific research relating to any other qualifying activities, the repair and maintenance of plant and machinery used in any manufacturing process, the repair of buildings used for any other qualifying activity, the systematic training of staff for work in qualifying activities.

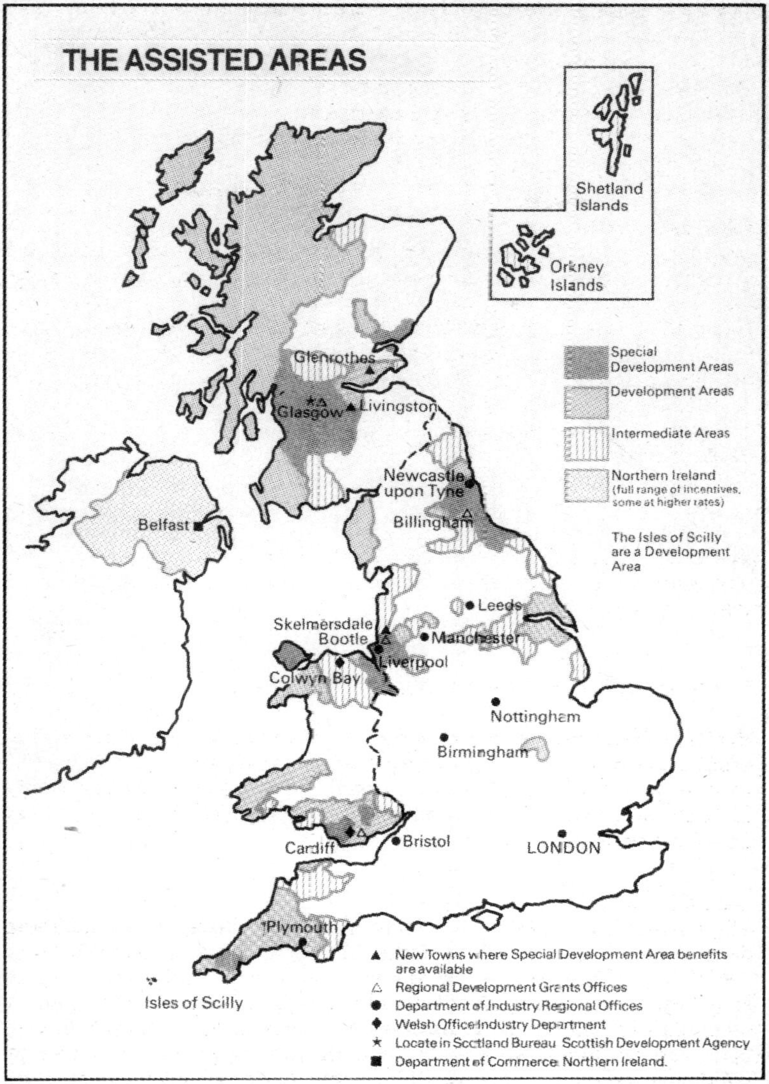
THE ASSISTED AREAS
Shetland Islands
Orkney Islands
Glenrothes
Glasgow
Livingston
Newcastle upon Tyne
Billingham
Belfast
Leeds
Skelmersdale
Bootle
Manchester
Liverpool
Colwyn Bay
Nottingham
Birmingham
Cardiff
Bristol
LONDON
Plymouth
Isles of Scilly
Special Development Areas
Development Areas
Intermediate Areas
Northern Ireland (full range of incentives, some at higher rates)
The Isles of Scilly are a Development Area
▲ New Towns where Special Development Area benefits are available
△ Regional Development Grants Offices
● Department of Industry Regional Offices
◆ Welsh Office Industry Department
★ Locate in Scotland Bureau Scottish Development Agency
■ Department of Commerce Northern Ireland.

Rate of grant payable

— Special Development Area	22% of cost
— Development Area	15% of cost

The grants are available towards capital expenditure on:

a Buildings — new individual buildings or works (excluding mining works), and extensions and adaptations of premises used wholly or mainly for qualifying activities.

The individual building scheme must cost £5,000 or more, and while the cost may include site preparation, it cannot include the cost of the site.

b Machinery and plant — individual items of new plant and machinery costing from £1,000 (£500 in the case of premises where less than 100 people are employed).

Second-hand items are not eligible for a grant, neither are vehicles other than mobile machinery or works vehicles.

Machinery and plant must be used for not less than one year, and have a useful life of at least four years. Things such as furniture, floor coverings, and decorative items are not eligible.

The grant is paid to the purchaser of the item, and this can include a hire-purchaser. Where the asset is being hired, as opposed to being bought, the grant is paid to the owner. There are special arrangements for sale-and-leaseback, and you should consult the Regional Development Grants office about these *before* applying for a grant.

How to apply

Applications for grants must be received by the appropriate Regional Development Grant Office within two years of the end of the quarter in which the asset was provided.

The addresses and telephone numbers of these Offices are to be found on page 161, and if you are in any difficulty about whether you are eligible for a grant you should consult with them at the earliest possible stage.

Any other considerations

Capital expenditure on plant and machinery anywhere in the UK qualifies for a first year tax allowance of 100%, Regional Development Grants are *not* deducted from the cost of the asset when these allowances are computed. In addition to this, these grants are not treated as income receipts for UK tax purposes and so they do not give rise to Corporation Tax.

Regional Development Grants are taken into account when considering Selective Financial Assistance (see page 184), and while it does not affect your eligibility for assistance under the scheme, it may influence the amount offered.

Selective financial assistance

As well as attracting Regional Development Grants, some businesses may also be eligible for Selective Financial Assistance. Broadly speaking, those businesses which create or safeguard jobs within the Assisted Areas can qualify for further help under Section 7 of the Industrial Development Act 1982. Selective Financial Assistance is administered by:

— Department of Industry
— Scottish Economic Planning Department
— Welsh Office Industry Department

Who qualifies?

Projects which are in the mining, manufacturing and construction industries may be eligible for assistance providing that they can demonstrate the following:

(i) Without the assistance the project could not go ahead in its proposed form, i.e. the provision of assistance must be shown to lead to:
— a significant change in the nature or scale of the project
— a significant advancement in its timing
— its location within an Assisted Area*

From this you can see that a project which has already started is unlikely to qualify, unless you can show that the assistance would significantly expand the project.

(ii) The project will lead to the creation of additional employment (Category A), or will safeguard existing jobs through modernisation (Category B).

Under Category A the project would be expected to create a specified number of jobs within three years (exceptionally five).
If the project only involves the transfer of jobs within Assisted Areas it is unlikely to qualify unless you can show that it is covered by Category B.

(iii) The project has a good prospect of being viable, and that the greater part of the finance required is to come from the private sector.

(iv) The project will contribute to the national economy, for example by improving productivity, increasing exports.

The effects on the industry as a whole, and on other UK producers will be taken into consideration.
Selective Financial Assistance usually takes the form of a grant paid in instalments, related to expenditure on fixed and working capital, and the achievement of the forecast objectives. Grants are discretionary and the amount and the term of the assistance is negotiated to provide the minimum amount necessary to enable the project to go ahead.

---

*This clause is known as the principle of 'Additionality'.

How to apply
If you think that you have a project which may be eligible under this scheme you should contact the Department of Industry for initial discussions. An early indication of whether or not your proposed application is likely to succeed could save you a great deal of work in preparing the necessary detailed documentation for such an application. You should *not* make any start on the project until an offer of assistance has been received.

Any other considerations
Other assistance which has been offered for the project, such as Regional Development Grants, will be taken into account when the amount of Selective Financial Assistance is being decided.

In-plant training scheme
This scheme was introduced to provide assistance towards the training costs which are part of an investment project in either the manufacturing or service industries. In order to qualify, training must be an essential part of the project, and a significant element in the cost of the project.

Who qualifies?
To be eligible for a grant the project must satisfy the same criteria as those laid down for Selective Financial Assistance.

Grant payable
The grant covers 40% of eligible training costs, which are: the basic wages of the trainees, the instructors, and cost of materials consumed. Where training takes place away from the normal place of work, the travel and subsistence expenses of the trainees and instructors may be included.
Training courses may last from 3–26 weeks (longer courses will only be considered in exceptional cases).

How to apply
Applications must be approved in advance, and information can be obtained from:
— Department of Industry
— Scottish Development Agency
— Welsh Office Industry Department.

Any other considerations
Projects which are eligible under this scheme may also be eligible for a further grant of 40% from the European Community.

Government factories

Within the Assisted Areas industrial and commercial premises may be available for sale or for rent for projects which create additional employment. In some cases existing businesses whose current premises are unsuitable may be re-housed.

Standard factory units of sizes ranging from small workshops of 500 sq.ft. to buildings of 25,000 sq.ft. are constructed, and all factories are built to as near a state of completion as possible. To cater for the needs of some of the new high technology industries some sites are being developed on or near to universities and polytechnics.

Although not strictly speaking a source of finance (rents are set at commercial levels), a rent-free period of up to 2 years may be available in some areas. Factories can also be bought, with capital and interest repayments spread over a period of up to 15 years at fixed rates of interest.

Businesses renting or buying government factories may also be eligible for Selective Financial Assistance, in which case they should apply for Selective Financial Assistance before making arrangements to occupy a factory. Any rental concessions will be taken into account when assessing the amount of Selective Financial Assistance to be given.

The factories are managed by the:

— English Industrial Estates Corporation
— Scottish Development Agency
— Welsh Development Agency.

Investment in office and service industries

If your business is part of the service sector as opposed to manufacturing industry, you will not have been eligible for a Regional Development Grant. Selective assistance is available for projects in those service industries covered by the Standard Industrial Classification Orders XXII–XXVI, and this includes most commercial, distributive and professional services. Projects which serve a purely local need e.g. the local corner shop, would not, however, normally be eligible.

Various departments of manufacturing, such as administration, marketing, training, research and development, would also be eligible providing they can be distinguished from the manufacturing activities which they service.

Who qualifies?

In order to qualify for a grant you must be able to show that:

— the project will create new jobs in an Assisted Area, either as a result of the business moving into the area, or if it is already established there, by undertaking a new project, or expanding an existing one.

— there is a genuine choice of location for the project between an Assisted Area and elsewhere in the UK. (Some firms which provide certain 'producer services' are exempt from this requirement.)
— without the assistance the project could not go ahead in its proposed form (i.e. the principle of Additionality).

Grant payable
The grant is based on the number of new jobs created by the project, and will be the minimum amount necessary for the project to go ahead.
The maximum grant available for each permanent job created is as follows:

— Special Development Area	£8,000
— Development Area	£5,000
— Intermediate Area	£2,500

50% of the grant is payable 12 months after the first job is created, the remaining 50% is payable 2 years later, or on completion of the project, whichever is the sooner. If the number of jobs created is below the number originally forecast, the second payment may be reduced accordingly.

Grants to key personnel
A fixed, non-taxable grant is available towards the expenses of an employee who moves with the firm into the Assisted Area. To be eligible he must have been employed by the firm for 6 months before the move, and stay with the firm for 6 months after the move.
The grant of £2,000 is made only if the removal expenses exceed £2,000, and a maximum of 30% of jobs can qualify for this grant.

Grant for feasibility study
In order to investigate the possibility of moving to an Assisted Area it may be necessary to commission a feasibility study from outside consultants. A grant of up to 25% of the consultants' fee, maximum £10,000, is available.

How to apply
Applications for grants must be made, and approval received, before starting the project. Further information about the scheme can be obtained from:
— Department of Industry
— Scottish Development Agency
— Welsh Development Agency.

Among the areas considered to have special problems Northern Ireland is regarded as a special case, and as such, there are a number of incentives available to firms setting up in business there. These incentives are in addition to many of the schemes available in other parts of the UK.

1. Automatic assistance
Automatic Assistance takes the form of grants which are available irrespective of the number of jobs which are to be created by a project. These schemes are administered by the Department of Economic Development.

Capital grants
These are similar to Regional Development Grants (page 110) in that they do not give rise to tax. A grant of 30% of eligible costs of new buildings, plant and machinery used for manufacturing purposes is available.

Training grants
Where employers provide training for additional workers to fill new jobs training grants are offered as follows:

— Employees aged 50 or over previously unemployed	£40 per week
— Employees aged 18–49	£30 per week
— Employees aged under 18	£20 per week

Government factories
New or second-hand factories can be bought or leased for industrial or commercial purposes other than retailing.

Rates relief
100% reduction on rates levied on industrial premises.

Key-workers grants
Where key-workers are transferred to Northern Ireland to help set up or expand a business there cash grants are available covering fares, lodging allowance, certain continuing liability expenses, and fares home. Loans and grants are provided for the purchase of new homes and removal expenses, and dependants' fares and professional expenses are fully reimbursed.

2. Selective assistance
Companies in the manufacturing and service industries which undertake new projects or expand existing operations may be eligible for further

assistance. These incentives are negotiable, and will be determined by the number of jobs that are to be created.

To qualify for Selective Assistance, projects must show that:

— they have a good prospect of being viable
— they will result in more productive and secure jobs (the 'efficiency' criterion)
— they can demonstrate the principle of additionality (see page 113).

Selective Assistance is administered by the Industrial Development Board.

Capital grants

The standard Automatic Assistance Capital Grant can be increased by negotiation up to a maximum of 50% of eligible capital costs. The rate of grant offered will depend on the location that the company chooses and the employment provided. The tax free element of the grant is limited to 45% of eligible costs.

Interest relief grants

Grants are made to offset the interest payments made when finance for new developments is raised through loans from non-government sources. Grants are available for up to 7 years, up to 3 years at a broadly commercial rate followed by 4 years at 3% per annum.

Rent grants

Grants contributing towards rent costs for both government or privately owned premises are available for up to 5 years.

Start-up grants

A substantial cash contribution may be made towards the setting-up cost incurred during the period in which a business is becoming established. This normally takes the form of an employment grant for each job created and is negotiated in relation to the total capital requirement. In addition, there are grants towards managerial costs, including salaries, during this period.

Venture capital

Equity participation can be made available to suit the needs of the particular project.

Corporation tax relief grant

A Corporation Tax Relief Grant of up to 80% will be granted to companies creating new employment. The grant will be availble by negotiation and is at the discretion of the Industrial Development Board and the Local Enterprise Development Unit.

Research and development grants
Grants of 40–50% are available towards labour and material costs of items such as basic research, related design work, making and testing of prototypes, final design and production drawing costs. Certain consultancy costs may also be eligible for assistance. Total grant available for any single project is £250,000.

Market research grants
Grants of up to 50% of the eligible costs involved in examining potential export markets are available. Eligible costs include consultants' fees and expenses, researchers' travel costs plus an allowance for in-house research and the purchase of market research of special marketing studies.
For further information about any of these schemes you should contact the following:

Department of Economic Development
Netherleigh
Massey Avenue
Belfast BT4 2JP
Tel: Belfast 63244

Industrial Development Board for Northern Ireland
IDB House
64 Chichester Street
Belfast BT1 4JX
Tel: Belfast 34488

Industrial Development Board for Northern Ireland
Ulster Office
11 Berkeley Street
London W1X 6BU
Tel: 01 493 0601

3. Local enterprise development unit
This is the small business agency for Northern Ireland and its basic aim is to promote the establishment of small local manufacturing and service industries employing less than 50 people. It does not normally assist wholesale, retail, distribution, tourist and transport operations, or industries not suited to small scale activities.
The Local Enterprise Development Unit can assist by making available:
— loans and grants geared to the needs of each project
— government factories and sites
— advice and practical help with marketing, accountancy and management problems

— a business centre for promotions and exhibitions, small business counselling and a licensing library

For further information on this Unit you should contact:

LEDU
Lamont House
Purdy's Lane
Newtonbreda
Belfast BT8 4TB
Tel: Belfast 691031

ENGLAND

1. The Development Commission

The Development Commission was established in 1909 *to assist the English rural areas*. In particular, the eight Commissioners advise the Government of the spending of the Development Fund, a sum voted annually by Parliament. The main aims of the Commission are to reduce rural de-population, improve the economic and social structure of the rural areas, and to create employment;

In setting out these objectives the Government recognised that some areas of the country were particularly disadvantaged, and designated these as Special Investment Areas. While, technically speaking, any scheme that would benefit the rural economy is eligible for assistance if no other statutory assistance is available, the Commission has concentrated the bulk of its resources on certain activities in the Special Investment Areas. These activities can be summarised into the following main categories:

— providing small factories and workshops in partnership with local authorities, both by building new units and by converting existing buildings
— providing assistance to small rural industries through the funding of the Council for Small Industries in Rural Areas (CoSIRA)
— encouraging voluntary organisations such as the Rural Community Councils, the National Council for Voluntary Organisations, and the National Federation of Women's Institutes, which enrich the social and cultural life of the rural areas

2. Council for small industries in rural areas (CoSIRA)

From the point of view of the small business, this is the most important aspect of the Development Commission's work. The Council for Small Industries in Rural Areas was established in 1968, and its job is to assist small firms employing not more than 20 skilled people in rural areas and country towns with a population of less than 10,000. In March 1983

CoSIRA was servicing some 13,400 rural small firms employing 72,000 people. Of the firms assisted 2,000 were new starters.

Loans

CoSIRA has its own loan fund for small industries and small tourist projects (agriculture, horticulture and the professions are not eligible).

The maximum loan available is £75,000, minimum £250, and this can cover up to 50% of the project cost on buildings, plant and equipment. Loans for buildings are made over a period of 20 years, and for plant and equipment 5 years; interest rates are specified by the Treasury and vary according to the term of the loan.

In addition to this CoSIRA have an agreement with the National Westminster Bank enabling clients to borrow up to £250,000 for buildings, plant and equipment.

Under a pilot scheme CoSIRA has been able to offer grants of up to 35% towards the conversion of redundant farm buildings in the Uplands. The Commission hopes to extend this scheme throughout the Special Investment Areas, and to all suitable buildings.

Designation of rural development areas

The Commission and CoSIRA have concentrated the bulk of their resources in the Special Investment Areas designated by the Government. Following a recent review the Commissioners are, in future, to designate their own priority areas, and these will be known as Rural Development Areas.

In deciding upon these areas the Commission will take into account such factors as:

— above average unemployment, and poor employment opportunities
— population decline, and the outward migration of people of working age
— imbalance in the age structure towards elderly people
— poor access to services and facilities.

It is intended that all the Rural Development Areas will be designated at the same time, probably in the first half of 1984.

For further information please contact:

The Development Commission
11 Cowley Street
London SW1P 3NA
Tel: 01 222 9134

CoSIRA
141 Castle Street
Salisbury
Wiltshire SP1 1EX
Tel: 0722 6255

3. British technology group (BTG)

The British Technology Group seeks to encourage the development of industrial projects in the Assisted Areas in England. It can provide long term investment funds, by way of share capital or loans, as well as joint venture finance and leasing. Financial packages are tailored to suit the needs of the applicant and are usually provided on normal commercial terms. Finance is provided to enable a project to go ahead and BTG will seek to withdraw from an investment when the project is well established. New ventures in the Assisted Areas with potential for long term growth, particularly those seeking to develop areas of advanced technology are likely to be considered by the BTG, which also has special schemes for small companies (Oakwood Loan Finance Ltd) and for innovative, technology based firms (Small Company Innovation Fund) throughout the whole of the UK.

Further information can be obtained from:

Marketing Division
British Technology Group
101 Newington Causeway
London SE1 6BU
Tel: 01 403 6666

SCOTLAND

1. Scottish Development Agency

As its name implies, the Scottish Development Agency is concerned with the promotion of the economic development of Scotland. Its objectives are to create and safeguard employment, increase industrial efficiency and international competitiveness, and to improve the environment. In order to achieve these aims, the Development Agency can give assistance in the form of loans, guarantees, share capital, industrial and financial partnerships, factories, and management advisory services.

While the Agency is prepared to consider any project in Scotland which comes within its general guidelines, the sort of projects which are most likely to be assisted are:

— projects already in Scotland, or about to be established there which plan to enter new markets or develop new techniques
— expansion projects by enterprise in Scotland
— companies in Scotland which have a good prospect of long term profitability but which are experiencing short term difficulties
— projects which will assist the economic regeneration of local economies.

Small business division

This division of the Agency can provide medium and long term loans of £1,000–£150,000 to small businesses in the manufacturing and service industries employing less than 100 people. The loans are generally for the following periods

5 years — plant, machinery, equipment, working capital

20 years — buildings

Security is usually required. Interest rates are fixed and will normally be at commercial levels, however, if your project will create additional employment in a rural area there may be some possibility of your being granted a concessionary rate.

In addition to providing finance, the Small Business Division also offers other services which might be of benefit to you:

- general counselling services
- advice on marketing, exporting, production organisation, materials, equipment, sub-contracting
- advice on financial management

(There may be a small charge for some of these services.)

The Scottish Development Agency acts as agent to the European Investment Bank and the European Coal and Steel Community and can make their loans available to businesses in Scotland.

Manufacturing businesses which create employment for redundant coal and steel workers in an area affected by closures can qualify for loans to cover 50% of the fixed capital costs of the project. Loans are given for a period of eight years, at fixed interest rates, with a four year repayment holiday. These loans are only available to firms with up to 50 employees.

For businesses which do not qualify under the Small Business Division's schemes the Development Agency can arrange loans for up to 20 years at competitive interest rates. There is no upper limit to the amount, but security will usually be required. The Development Agency may also be prepared to give guarantees, on suitable terms, to enable businesses to borrow money from other sources.

Finance provided by the Scottish Development Agency is regarded as coming from the private sector, and therefore does not affect the regional assistance available under the Assisted Areas.

Information on the above, including the Small Business Division can be obtained from:

Information Department
Scottish Development Agency
120 Bothwell Street
Glasgow G2 7JP
Tel: 041 248 2700

2. Highlands and Islands Development Board

This Government agency was established in 1965 to assist the economic and social development of the Scottish Highlands and Islands.

The Board can provide finance in the form of loans, grants and equity for a wide range of developments in the following areas: the Highland Region, the Western Isles, Shetland, Orkney and, in Strathclyde Region, Argyll and Bute District, the Isle of Arran and Cumbrae.

Projects moving from non-development areas into one of the above may qualify for a grant of 80% of removal costs.

The type of projects which the Board is prepared to consider for assistance include those in the manufacturing industry, crafts, tourist facilities, agriculture and fishing.

Finance

The amount available in loans and grants is discretionary and will depend upon such factors as location and the employment created. The Board is able to offer 50% of the total cost of establishing the project, the other half being provided by the entrepreneur from his own resources or from commercial borrowing. In exceptional circumstances the Board can provide up to 70% of the finance required.

Loans are provided for up to 10 years for plant, machinery and working capital, and for up to 20 years for buildings. Rates of interest are fixed and may be below commercial levels. Although security is usually required, the Board has the discretionary power to waive this for loans of up to £6,000.

As an alternative to giving loans, the Board can make available interest relief grants to reduce the interest costs of borrowing from other sources.

'Special Grants' are available for projects which the Board considers have particular significance, and which could not go ahead without additional help. These grants are normally of up to 20% of the project's costs (in exceptional cases this can be extended to 50% where the project cost is less than £60,000).

The usual Regional Development Grants are available throughout most of the Highlands and Islands, and the Board would expect them to be taken up. Such grants will be taken into account when determining the level of assistance to be given by the Highlands and Islands Board.

Other services provided by the Board include:

— Social Development Grants

  Grants of up to £12,000 are available towards projects that meet social needs, and contribute to social development.

— Training Grants.

  New companies or existing businesses which recruit new staff may be eligible for grants of up to 50% of the identifiable training costs.

— Factories.
Standard and custom built factories are available at favourable rents, and in some cases, rent free for up to 2 years.
— Advisory Services
The Board provides an advisory service which can cover such subjects as marketing, production engineering, management accounting, recruitment and training.

The address of the Highlands and Islands Development Board is:

The Highlands and Islands Development Board
Bridge House
Bank Street
Inverness IV1 1QR
Tel: 0463 34171

3. Clydebank Enterprise Fund

New businesses setting up within the area covered by the Clydebank Enterprise Zone are eligible for loans from this Fund. It provides unsecured risk finance for loans of up to £25,000 at a rate of interest of 5%.

4. Local enterprise grants for urban projects

The first round of a pilot scheme to provide assistance to projects in deprived urban areas was announced in September 1982. Although the closing date for the scheme is now passed, further rounds are to be considered in the future and it may be worth keeping an eye on the press for any indication of further rounds.

Any type of project which will bring benefit to a deprived urban area, and which can demonstrate additionality was eligible under the rules of the first round.

The pilot scheme was administered by the Scottish Development Agency.

WALES

1. Mid Wales Development

The Mid Wales Development offers finance, business advice and other services to encourage firms to set up, or expand their operations in Wales.

The areas it covers are:

Dyfed —	Ceredigion
Gwynedd —	Merionnydd
Powys —	Brecknock
	Montgomery
	Radnor

The Mid Wales Development can offer the following:

Rural loans
Loans up to £50,000 are available to firms employing less than 20 skilled people, the loans being dependent on the creation of sufficient new jobs. Interest rates are fixed, and are at approx. 3% below commercial rates, security is normally required.

Standard loans
Loans ranging from £2,500 to £500,000 are available for projects at commercial fixed interest rates. The loans are available for buildings, plant and machinery, and working capital, with repayment terms of 5–20 years. Priority is given to manufacturing industry, and projects within the transport, distribution, construction, agriculture and retails sectors are not eligible.
Equity finance can also be provided usually as part of a package including standard loans.
Applications must be made before the start of the project.

Wage subsidy
Small firms (employing 25 people or less) may obtain a wage subsidy of up to 30% of the basic wage on up to 5 new jobs. The jobs must be filled by previously unemployed people, and the subsidy is paid for 26 weeks. The subsidy is at the discretion of the local council.

Mid Wales Development grants
Grants are available for projects in the manufacturing, commercial, construction and service industries which create or safeguard jobs in areas which lost their Assisted Area status. The criteria for grants are similar to those for Selective Assistance in Assisted Areas (page 000), and projects must show that without the grant the scheme could not go ahead. It follows, therefore, that applications should be made before the start of the project.

Factories
Factories of between 500 and 20,000 sq.ft. are available in many towns, and rent-free periods of up to 2 years will be considered depending on the area.

Business Advisory Service
A Business Advisory Service gives guidance on marketing, promotions, accountancy and setting up in business.

2. Welsh Development Agency

The Welsh Development Agency was established in 1976 to help regenerate the Welsh economy by providing investment funds, factories and advisory services to assist both new and existing industries.

Loans

Investment capital in the form of equity funds and loans is provided and financial packages are designed to meet the needs of individual businesses. All sectors of industry, with the exception of property development, financial businesses and service industries meeting only a local need, are eligible.

Loans are made on commercial terms, usually for a period of 5–10 years, at fixed rates of interest. Deferrment of capital repayments can be arranged, and security is usually required. Small businesses which create new jobs in rural areas may qualify for loans at reduced rates of interest. It is the Agency's policy to limit its shareholdings to 30% of the equity of any company, and it negotiates buy-back arrangements for the subsequent disposal of holdings on agreed terms.

Hafren Investment Finance Ltd

Hafren Investment Finance is a venture capital subsidiary of the Development Agency which specialises in providing risk funds for new technology projects and young companies with a high growth potential. £10,000–£100,000 is available per business, and Hafren will allow an early buy out of its stake on terms agreed at the start.

Small Business Unit

The Small Business Unit of the Agency provides management and technical advice to small firms. These services are charged for on a sliding scale according to company size.

Other services:

— Factories
  The Welsh Development Agency builds standard and custom built factories ranging from 400 sq.ft. to 50,000 sq.ft.
— General Advice
  The Development Agency can provide information and advice on the grants and loans available to businesses in Wales. Information on labour, materials, suppliers, housing etc. is also available.

European assistance

The Development Agency acts as agent for the European Investment Bank and the European Coal and Steel Community. Low interest loans are available to businesses in the Assisted Areas, and to manufacturing firms in the areas affected by closures in the coal and steel sectors.

Mid Wales Development
Ladywell House
Newtown
Powys
SY16 1JB
Tel: 0686 26965

Welsh Development Agency
Pontypridd
Mid Glamorgan
CF37 5UT
Tel: 044 385 2666

FUNDS FROM THE EUROPEAN ECONOMIC COMMUNITY

The Community's budget provides for a number of funds which are designed to promote the Community's objectives by financing suitable projects, such funds include the Social Fund and the Regional Development Fund. In addition to these, there are specialised Community institutions such as the European Investment Bank (EIB), which provides finance in the form of grants and low interest loans for projects mainly in the industrial, energy and infrastructure fields.
The regulations governing the operations of these funds and institutions can be complex, and are designed to ensure that the finance is used to achieve the objectives of the Community. As the Community's policies and objectives change, the regulations are reviewed and up-dated, additionally the money allocated to these funds has to be voted by the member states every year, and consequently the amount of cash available can vary.
However, the EEC could be a very useful source of finance for you to consider, and you should not be put off by the apparent remoteness of Brussels, a number of the schemes which are likely to be of most interest to the small business are administered by more local institutions acting as agents for the Community.

1. The European Investment Bank (EIB)
The European Investment Bank was established to provide funds in the form of loans and guarantees for capital investment projects in industry, energy, tourism or related infrastructure or services.
To do this the EIB raises money on the world's money markets and then on-lends these funds at fixed interest rates. Because of its status as a

borrower it is able to obtain money at the best rates, and can offer loans at advantageous rates of interest.

Since the UK joined the EEC in 1973, the EIB has provided public and private sector borrowers in Britain with loans totalling over £2,700 million.

The loans are usually made in a mixture of currencies and the borrower repays them in the same currencies. Exchange rate movements can, therefore, increase or decrease the sterling value of the repayments. To avoid this uncertainty, the UK Government operates exchange risk guarantee schemes for both the public and private sector which fixes the borrower's liability in sterling.

In the UK a project may be eligible for EIB assistance if it:

— promotes regional development in the Assisted Areas;

or

— serves a common interest of several Member States or the Community as a whole;

or

— leads to the modernisation or conversion of industries to overcome structural problems.

The majority of loans are made for industrial investment, the development of energy supplies (particularly those which reduce the EEC's dependence on oil imports), and the improvement of public infrastructure.

Loans from the EIB are made in two ways:

— Direct Loans

— Agency and Global Loans

Direct loans

These loans are negotiated directly between the EIB and the prospective borrower. The lower limit of the loans is usually £1.5m.

Agency and global loans

In order to make money available to smaller borrowers the EIB makes global loans available to banks and other financial institutions. These institutions act as intermediaries and on-lend the funds in amounts which would be too small for the EIB to deal with directly. Agency loans are made via departments of the UK government.

Normally companies with net assets of less than £45m and fewer than 500 employees will be eligible. Loans are available for projects within the mining, quarrying, manufacturing, processing, packaging, tourist and some service industries.

The loans cover 50% of the cost of capital expenditure, and you must provide the remaining half yourself from other sources. Repayments are normally over 8 years (10 years for agency loans for tourist projects), and

are made in half-yearly instalments of capital and interest. An initial deferment of 2 years may be available on the capital repayments. Interest rates are fixed at the time of borrowing, and in the case of loans from the EIB's global funds will include a charge for Exchange Risk Cover, and, where applicable the risk the intermediary carries in guaranteeing the loan to the EIB.
Who to contact:

(i) *Assisted Areas*
Agency loans from £15,000–£4.5m
English regional offices of the Department of Industry
Scottish Economic Planning Department
Welsh Office Industry Department
Northern Ireland Industrial Development Board
Northern Ireland Local Enterprise Development Unit
English, Scottish and Wales Tourist Boards

Loans from £15,000–£2m
Industrial and Commercial Finance Corporation
Midland Bank

Loans from £15,000–£250,000
Scottish Development Agency
Welsh Development Agency
Clydesdale Bank
National Westminster Bank

(ii) *Outside the Assisted Areas*
Loans from £15,000–£250,000
Industrial and Commercial Finance Corporation
Midland Bank
National Westminster Bank

2. Exchange Risk Guarantee Scheme
Loans from the EIB and the ECSC are usually made in foreign currencies. In order to cover private sector borrowers against the risk of exchange losses the Government operates an Exchange Risk Guarantee Scheme.
Projects which meet the criteria for Regional Selective Financial Assistance are eligible for the scheme whereby the Government takes the risk in return for an annual premium, and the borrowers liability is fixed in sterling. Finance provided under the global loans facility is automatically provided with Exchange Risk cover, in the case of agency loans you should contact the Government department concerned.

3. European Social Fund

The European Social Fund is essentially concerned with employment and training, and operates by giving financial support in the form of grants to training schemes which meet specified conditions. A grant from the Social Fund to a private sector firm can match, but not exceed assistance already being provided by the public authority. In general, assistance is given for the running costs of schemes, and will not cover capital expenditure.

Following the recent review of the work of the Fund it seems clear that the bulk of its resources will be directed towards assisting schemes which will promote employment for young people under 25, whose chances of employment are particularly poor through lack of training, or who are long term unemployed.

Applications to the Fund should be channelled through the Department of Employment which will provide guidelines and application forms.

The Fund is heavily oversubscribed and not all eligible schemes will necessarily receive funding.

4. European Coal and Steel Community (ECSC)

Funds from the ECSC are made available to projects which promote the modernisation of the coal and steel industries, and which provide employment opportunities for redundant coal and steel workers.

Conversion loans

Firms in the manufacturing industries which undertake projects which will create employment opportunities for redundant coal and steel workers may qualify for grants of up to 50% of the fixed capital costs of the project. To be eligible the firm does not have to be related to the coal and steel industries, but must be located within an affected area. This is usually taken to mean within a radius of 10–15 miles of a steel works or coal mine where there have been redundancies.

Loans are made at fixed rates of interest, usually for a term of 8 years. Capital repayment holidays can be arranged, and *interest relief of up to 3% per annum may be granted,* depending on the number of jobs created and the location. Exchange risk cover can be arranged.

Applications for a grant must be made before work starts on a project, and details can be obtained from:

— Department of Industry
— Scottish Economic Planning Department
— Welsh Office Industry Department
— Northern Ireland Department of Economic Planning

How to Apply

— for loans of £4m or more application should be made via the Department of Industry
— for loans of up to £1m apply to the Industrial and Commercial Finance Corporation
  Scottish Development Agency
  Welsh Development Agency
  Clearing banks

Industrial loans

Loans similar to the above can be given to projects involving investment in plant, machinery and buildings which reflect Community Policy for coal and steel. Any project which assists the use of coal and steel e.g. by increasing production, reducing costs, can be eligible, and finance is not restricted to the coal and steel industries themselves.
Application should be made as indicated above.

Housing loans

Loans at low rates of interest are available for improving the housing conditions of workers in the coal and steel industries, both for new construction and modernisation.
The maximum loan for first time buyers is 20% of the purchase cost, up to 25% for transferees, and up to 40% for improvements. The cost of the loans is 1.75% including a commission to the Building Society which operated the scheme for the Commission.
Applications for the loans are made via your employers, and further details can be obtained from:

European Communities Commission
Information Office
8 Storey's Gate
London
SW1P 3AT
Tel: 01-222-8122

Other Assistance

Grants for research in the coal and steel industry are available for technical, economic, social and medical research projects.
Grants to coal and steel workers affected by fundamental change in market conditions can be given to help resettlement in other regions and training.
Further information can be obtained from the above address.

5. European Regional Development Fund (ERDF)
The ERDF was established in 1975 to assist Regional Development. The 'quota' section of the fund is used to assist projects in industry, tourism, service activities and infrastructure within the Assisted Areas. The project must also be receiving funds from the UK government.
The Department of Industry and its equivalents in Scotland, Wales and Northern Ireland administer the scheme.
The 'non-quota' section can provide assistance to small and medium sized firms (manufacturing firms with less than 200 employees, other firms with less than 25) who are engaged in certain activities within areas affected by the restructuring of the steel and ship building areas.
The areas affected are Strathclyde, Cleveland, Tyne and Wear, Merseyside, Corby, Clwyd, South Glamorgan, West Glamorgan, Gwent and Belfast.

The activities eligible for assistance include:

— provision of consultancy and common services
— promoting technological innovation, providing information on innovation
— facilitating access to risk capital

Details of the assistance available should be sought from:

Department of Industry
Regional Policy and Development Grants Division
Kingsgate House
66–74 Victoria Street
London SW1E 6SJ
Tel: 01 212 0400

6. European energy sector funds
The European Community has allocated funds for the promotion of more efficient energy installation and for the encouragement of a higher level of technological innovation.

Assistance is available for projects in the following fields:
— nuclear energy
— hydrocarbons
— uranium prospecting
— alternative energy
— energy saving projects

Details of these schemes can be obtained from the European Community Commission.

LOCAL AUTHORITIES

Your Local Authority could be a very useful source of finance to you, and it is one that is frequently overlooked, so it is worthwhile contacting them to find out what sort of assistance they can offer in your area. Because they vary considerably in the scope and type of schemes which they offer, it is possible to give only a broad outline here; for fuller information you should ask your Local Authority to send you any pamphlets or publications on local schemes.

All Local Authorities have certain general powers to provide assistance to industry where this is in the local interest. These powers include the giving of mortgage loans of up to 90% for buying land, or carrying out works on land; with the permission of the Secretary of State they may dispose of land at below its market value (this is only done in exceptional circumstances); and Local Authorities may invest monies from their pension funds in local businesses.

Within the guidelines laid down by the various statutes, the Local Authorities are able to set their own priorities in allocating resources, and this means that the amount of money available differs from area to area. The criteria by which applications for assistance are assessed will also be given different weight by the individual Authorities according to their priorities, so it is important that you should be aware of the particular policies of the Authority covering the area in which you wish to establish your business.

In addition to the general powers described above many Local Authorities have obtained additional powers through Private Acts of Parliament. These powers enable them to draw up their own schemes to assist local businesses, and there is a wide variety of such schemes available throughout the UK. It is impossible to list the individual schemes here due to their number and complexity, but your local Town Hall should be able to tell you if there are any such schemes in your area.

The most common Local Authority schemes cover the following:

— Wage subsidies and grants given to firms recruiting the unemployed. Subsidies are usually available for a specified length of time, and the Authority will have guidelines on how long the recruit must have been unemployed to qualify, and the minimum number of hours per week he must work to be eligible.

— Factories. Local Authorities are often able to provide premises with subsidised rents, or short term leases. Premises such as workshops suitable for small enterprises are being made available in increasing numbers.

— Loans and grants for working capital. Most Local Authority finance is specifically reserved for providing premises, however, some Authorities have schemes for plant and working capital, and these usually take the form of loans of up to 90% of the cost.

— Relocation grants. Some Authorities provide grants towards the cost of relocation, usually with a maximum of £2,000.
— Start-Up and Small Business Schemes. Start-up schemes often take the form of a package including loans, guarantees, workshop facilities. Small Business schemes are designed to encourage small businesses, (Local Authority definitions of 'small business' vary, usually between 5–10 people) and grants are available up to about £2,000.

1. Inner urban areas
Section 1 of the Inner Urban Areas Act 1978 defines certain districts which are known as Designated Districts. These are areas which have had special 'inner city' problems, and the Local Authorities at county and borough district levels are empowered to provide additional financial assistance to businesses in those areas. Priority is usually given to manufacturing industry, but projects from the service sector may also be considered.

Who qualifies?
Before giving assistance under these schemes your Local Authority would have to be satisfied that your business would:
— benefit the economic development of the particular area
— be viable, and either create or preserve jobs
— where appropriate, lead to improvements in either property or the environment
— not be able to obtain the necessary finance from other sources.

Assistance available
— loans of up to 90% of the secured value (i.e. mortgage loans) for buying land and for carrying out building and site works. Loans are available for up to 30 years at commercial rates of interest.
— grants or loans of up to £1,000 towards the costs of setting up co-operatives or common ownership enterprises.
This can only cover the administrative costs e.g. registration fees, professional advice, but not capital or running costs.
— the Local Authority can declare certain places 'Improvement Areas' in order to provide loans and grants for improvements to amenities in commercial or industrial areas which would otherwise decline due to poor buildings and environment.
Grants are available covering 50% of the cost of converting, improving and modernising commercial and industrial buildings.

Some of the Designated Districts have 'inner city partnership areas' within which are certain defined areas, known as Special Areas where the

Local Authority can provide additional assistance:
- interest free loans for up to 2 years for site preparation and the installation of services
- grants to assist with rents paid by firms taking leases on buildings for industrial or commercial use
- grants towards the interest being paid by firms employing less than 50 people on loans made for the purpose of buying land or buildings.
  To be eligible the firm must have been trading in the Special Area for 12 months, and the maximum grant is 12% of the amount borrowed. The grant can be paid in instalments over up to 4 years, but you cannot receive more than 6% of total sum borrowed in any one year.

The individual Authorities can set the terms and conditions of the assistance that they offer. Generally speaking, interest rates on loans are usually at commercial rates and security will be required. Assistance may be made conditional on certain employment creation targets being met, or standards of wages or working conditions being achieved.

How to apply
Application procedures are laid down by the individual Authorities and you should seek guidance from them on the correct way to apply. Because of the variations between the Local Authorities, both in interpretation and implementation of the schemes you are strongly advised to contact them as soon as is practicable to get an indication of whether your project is likely to be given consideration.

2. Enterprise zones
Enterprise Zones were originally created as an experiment to assess to what extent industrial and commercial activity would be encouraged by the lifting of certain tax burdens, and the relaxation of some administrative and statutory controls.
New and existing businesses within the designated Zones can benefit from the following concessions:
- exemption from rates on industrial and commercial property
- exemption from Development Land Tax
- 100% allowances for Income and Corporation Tax purposes on industrial and commercial property
- simplification of planning procedures
- government requests for statistical information will be reduced to a minimum
- exemption from Industrial Training Board levies, as well as any requirements to supply them with information

The special incentives in Enterprise Zones are in addition to whatever other benefits may be available under other schemes e.g. Assisted Area schemes.

The areas currently designated as Enterprise Zones are:

England	Corby, Dudley, Hartlepool, Isle of Dogs, Newcastle/Gateshead, Speke, Salford/Trafford, Wakefield.
Scotland	Clydebank
Wales	Lower Swansea Valley
Northern Ireland	Belfast

It has now been announced that additional enterprise Zones are to be established, and the new Zones will be:

England	Middlesborough, NE Lancashire, NW Kent, Rotherham, Scunthorpe, Telford, Wellingborough, Allerdale.
Scotland	Invergordon, Arbroath/Dundee
Wales	Flint, Milford Haven
Northern Ireland	Londonderry

3. Urban Development Corporations
Two Urban Development Corporations have been set up in the dockland areas of London and Merseyside to assist in the regeneration of these areas. They have been given special powers to undertake programmes of land acquisition and infrastructure provision in order to attract private sector development.
Their powers to provide loans and grants are similar to those of the local authorities in the Designated Districts.

For more information on the Corporations you should contact:

London Dockland Development Corporation
West India House
Millwall Dock
London E14 9TL
Tel: 01 515 3000

Merseyside Development Corporation
Royal Liver Building
Pier Head
Liverpool L3 1JE
Tel: 051 236 6090

1. TOURISM

Discretionary assistance for projects which provide or improve tourist facilities throughout the UK are available from the English, Welsh and Scottish Tourist Boards. Each Board has its own priorities and operates its own schemes so the assistance available will vary.

In general terms, the Boards will be prepared to consider projects which will attract more tourists both from Britain and from abroad, will increase tourist spending, and will create employment directly or indirectly.

The assistance is available towards capital costs only, and projects must, where required, have already been granted outline planning permission. To qualify for a grant you must be able to demonstrate that your project is viable, and that it could not go ahead in its proposed form without the assistance i.e. Additionality. The level of assistance will be limited to the minimum amount necessary to enable the project to proceed.

Grants can be of up to 50% of the capital costs of the project, although in practice they are usually in the region of 25–30%.

To encourage greater private sector finance the Tourist Boards also offer Interest Relief Grants for tourist development projects. These grants reduce the cost of borrowing for up to 3 years (exceptionally 4 years), and are currently as follows:

— first and second years 11%
— third and fourth years 3%

The Relief Grants can provide for borrowings of up to 50% of the costs for new projects, and up to 75% of the costs of extensions to existing businesses.

For small hotels, guest houses etc. in certain rural areas and country towns in the Special Development and Development Areas, and in the Development Commission's Special Investment Areas, loans may be available from the Council for Small Industries in Rural Areas (CoSIRA).

Assistance for a project can be a combination of the above grants and loans from other public funds, but the total assistance given can not exceed 50% of the total capital cost. Any assistance in excess of £50,000 (currently under review) must first be approved by the Department of Trade, the Welsh Office or the Scottish Economic Planning Department, and the Treasury.

The Tourist Boards act as agents for the European Investment Bank (EIB), and projects in the Assisted Areas may be eligible for loans of up to £2.5m.

The Highlands and Islands Development Board also provides assistance to tourist projects within its region.

The addresses of the Tourist Boards are as follows:

English Tourist Board
4 Grosvenor Gardens
London SW1W 0DU
Tel: 01 730 3400

Scottish Tourist Board
23 Ravelston Terrace
Edinburgh EH4 3EU
Tel: 031 332 2433

Wales Tourist Board
Brunel House
2 Fitzalan Road
Cardiff CF2 1UY
Tel: 0222 499909

TRANSPORT

Rail freight facilities grant
A grant of up to 50% (exceptionally 60%) is available to companies toward the capital cost of freight facilities where it can be shown that the investment will ensure that freight will be transferred to, or maintained on the railways.
The project must improve the environment for local communities, and must also demonstrate Additionality.

For further information contact:
Freight Services Officer
British Railways Board
222 Marylebone Road
London NW1 6JJ
Tel: 01 262 3232

Inland waterways freight facilities grant
A grant similar to the above, relating to inland waterways freight facilities, such as inland waterways terminals, depots, access roads.
For further information contact:
Department of Transport
2 Marsham Street
London SE1P 3EB
Tel: 01 212 8294/8168/7118

New bus grant
The Department of Transport may make a grant to any public service vehicle operator in England, Scotland and Wales towards the purchase price of approved buses for use wholly or mainly for stage services.

Fuel duty rebate
A refund of 100% of the duty charged on fuel used on stage carriage services is available to public service vehicle operators in England, Scotland and Wales. Express services, tours and contract work are not eligible.
For information on both of the above you should contact:

Department of Transport
PTI Division
2 Marsham Street
London SW1P 2EB
Tel: 01 212 7490

For Northern Ireland a Fuel Duty Rebate is available similar to the above, New Bus Grants are available only to specified operators.

Department of the Environment (NI)
Transport Division
Hampden House
55 Royle Avenue
Belfast BT1 1TX
Tel: Belfast 221212

NATION-WIDE SCHEMES

Research, development and new technology
In recent years there has been an increasing emphasis on the need for investment in research and development, particularly that related to the new technologies.
The Department of Industry is encouraging innovation and the exploitation of new technology with a number of special schemes designed to promote the use of computers, microprocessors and fibre-optics. As well as providing general advice and expert knowledge some of these schemes offer financial assistance towards the costs of equipment and project costs.
The British Technology Group also provides funds for firms involved in these areas.

1. Support for innovation
The aim of this scheme is to help companies in, or closely associated with any UK manufacturing industry to get new, or significantly improved products on to the market quickly, and more effectively. Projects which

involve innovation in traditional sectors as well as those dealing with new technology are eligible for assistance under the scheme.

To be eligible for support you must be able to show that:

— the company has the managerial, commercial, financial and technical ability to carry the project through
— the development has a good prospect of success
— without the government assistance the project could not proceed in its proposed form i.e. Additionality

Support will be given throughout the development, from the design stage to the launch, and the eligible costs will be the attributable labour, materials and overhead costs incurred up to the point of commercial production. These costs can include consultancy fees, design costs and prototypes.

The cost of the project should normally fall into the range of £25,000–£5m, however, small firms are encouraged to submit plans costing below the £25,000. Any other government assistance being provided towards the project e.g. Regional Development Grant will be deducted from eligible costs before an offer of assistance under this scheme is made.

Approval must be obtained before the work is commenced, no retrospective assistance will be given.

The support can take the form of:

Grants

Grants of up to $33\frac{1}{3}\%$ of the eligible costs can be given.

Shared cost contracts

For longer term projects, and usually only in exceptional circumstances, the Department of Industry may participate in a shared cost contract where it will bear up to 50% of eligible costs. This investment is recovered by a levy on commercial sales.

Pre-production models

Under a pre-production order agreement the Department of Industry may purchase up to 4 pre-production models which embody the new techniques, and will place these with potential users for evaluation.

The trial period usually lasts for one year, at the end of which the user is expected to buy the product if it is satisfactory. If the product is not satisfactory the Department will expect the manufacturer to buy back the equipment at an agreed price, allowing for depreciation.

The orders should normally total between £25,000 and £1.25m, but again, orders of less than £25,000 will be welcomed from small firms.

Applicants for this support will be expected to explain why adequate sales and trials cannot be achieved without government aid.

For further details contact:

Technology Policy Unit
Department of Industry
29 Bressenden Place
London SW1E 5DT
Tel: 01 213 3950

2. Joint appraisal scheme

Companies which are applying for government aid towards research and development costs may also be seeking funds from banks and other financial institutions. Where the Department of Industry has made an offer of assistance under the Support for Innovation it will make its technical appraisal of the project available to financial institutions to help in the assessment of possible cooperation in the joint promotion of the project.

For further information contact:

Dept. of Industry
MAP Office
Room 433
29 Bressenden Place
London SW1E 5DT
Tel: 01 213 6218

3. Computer-Aided design/computer-aided manufacturing (CADCAM)

The Government has recognised that the computer has great potential for increasing productivity and competitiveness, and in 1982 it launched an awareness campaign to accelerate the acceptance and application of computer aids to design, draughting, planning, estimating and manufacturing. CADCAM is directed principally at the mechanical and engineering sectors.

Under the scheme the following assistance is available to firms.

Support for consultancy studies

A grant of up to £2,000 is available on a selective basis towards the cost of a consultant to investigate the economic or technical feasibility of using computer aids. Grants are limited to one per firm, and the Department of Industry must approve the choice of consultant and the CADCAM project before the study commences.

Support for product and process development

Grants are available on the same terms as Support for Innovation (see above).

Demonstration firms
Firms with CADCAM installations who are willing to demonstrate their systems to potential users may receive support.
Other Assistance:
— Managers Awareness Seminars
One day CADCAM seminars including case studies and discussions with a consultant for managing directors.
— In-Depth Courses
One week courses to help design managers and production managers plan their firm's approach to the technology
— Practical Experience Centres
CADCAM centres provide facilities so that key staff from potential users can study techniques and try out the equipment.
— CADCAM Information Point
An information point is being set up to provide information on equipment, suppliers, software, courses etc.
Information on CADCAM can be obtained from any Department of Industry Regional Office, or:

Department Of Industry
MEE2 Branch
Room 401
Ashdown House
123 Victoria Street
London SW1E 6RB
Tel: 01 212 5789

4. Computer aided design manufacture and test (CADMAT)
In the production of computers and electronic equipment there are specialist requirements for the design, verification, layout and interconnection of circuits, and for manufacture, procurement and testing. The computer aided techniques designed to satisfy these requirements are known as CADMAT. The CADMAT programme is designed at extending and accelerating the use of CADMAT by small and medium sized firms, and is directed mainly at the electronics industry.

Development costs
Grants of up to $33\frac{1}{3}\%$ of eligible costs are available to support the development of CADMAT tools and standards which benefit the UK electronics industry. Applications should be made before 31 May 1984.

Capital support grants
First time users of modern CADMAT equipment can apply for a grant of up to $33\frac{1}{3}\%$ towards the cost of hardware, software, installation and the training of personnel where such a grant will accelerate the introduction

of the equipment. Software houses or bureaux which provide direct design or test support to the manufacturing industry may also be eligible for support.

For further information on the above grants contact:

Electronics Application Division
Department of Industry
29 Bressenden Place
London
SW1E 5DT
Tel: 01 213 7404

Other assistance

— Seminars for Management
Seminars for top management organised by the Institution of Electrical Engineers to promote awareness of CADMAT.

— Short Courses
Two day courses to give managers and engineers a knowledge of the basics needed to use CADMAT.

— Demonstrations
Major users of CADMAT are to put on demonstrations to show how the system works in the actual industrial environment.

— Information Service
The Department of Industry has set up an information service on all aspects of the technology for the benefit of existing and prospective CADMAT users.

For further information on these services contact:

The Institution of Electrical Engineers
Savoy Place
London WC2R 0BL
Tel: 01 240 1871

5. Computer aided design and test equipment (CADTES)

Capital equipment purchases in support of computer aided design; manufacture and test schemes can be provided to first time users of computer aided application. The eligible costs include any mixture of hardware and software purchase or leasing cost (4 year minimum lease) plus an allowance of up to 15% for training and installation costs.

The grant of up to 33⅓% of eligible costs is subject to a maximum of £60,000 to any one firm. There is no lower limit for firms employing up to 200 people, larger firms are subject to a minimum of £6,000.

Applications for this assistance must be made before 31 July 1984.

Notes for the guidance of applicants should be obtained from:
Electronics Application Division
Department of Industry
29 Bressenden Place
London SW1E 5DT
Tel: 01 213 7404

6. Software products scheme
This scheme was established in 1973 to encourage the development of software products and packages and their practical application in key technological areas. Any UK based software company, bureau or consultancy can apply for a grant of up to 33⅓% of the cost of developing and marketing the product in the first two years. Proposals can be for a new product or for the further development of an existing one.
For further information contact:
The Software Products Scheme Administrator
The National Computing Centre Ltd
Oxford Road
Manchester M1 7ED
Tel: 061 228 6333

7. Telecoms Products Scheme
This scheme provides grants for product development and capital equipment and applies to equipment designed to be attached to public telecommunications networks. It is aimed particularly at small to medium sized firms and grants of up to 33⅓% for development, and negotiable grants for capital equipment are available, where the total project cost does not exceed £3m.
Applications must be received within six months of government approval of the appropriate BSI standard.
For further information contact:
Department of Industry
Information Technology Division
Room 521
29 Bressenden Place
London SW1E 5DT
Tel: 01 213 6505 and 6515

8. Microelectronics industry support programme
Assistance can be given, on a selective basis, to promote investment in the manufacture of microelectronic components and to encourage research and development of both products and processes.

All firms engaged in the manufacture of microelectronic components and those firms supplying specialised equipment, materials or services to the industry may be eligible. In order to qualify, research and development projects must cost a minimum of £10,000, and capital investment projects £25,000.
In addition, you must also be able to show that:
— the company is viable, and has the technical and financial capability to carry through the project
— the project must have a good prospect of success and significantly improve the company's performance
— the project could not take place at all, or within a reasonable time-scale without the government support
A grant of up to 33⅓% of qualifying costs for research and development, and investment in production facilities is available. In the case of research and development projects support is available in the form of a shared-cost contract of up to 50% of total qualifying project costs, recoverable by a levy on related sales.
Applications for assistance must be made before a project is started, and in time for completion by 31 March 1985.

Department of Industry
Electronics Applications Division
29 Bressenden Place
London SW1E 5DT
Tel: 01 213 5836

9. Microprocessor application project
The aim of this project is to encourage UK industry to apply microprocessor technology to a wide range of products and production processes.
Selective assistance is available to all sectors of UK manufacturing industry in the following ways.

Industrial training and awareness
The Department of Industry will assist with the cost of developing training courses designed to train engineers in the use of microelectronics. The rate of grant will usually be 50% of allowable costs for public courses, 25% for in-house courses.

Feasibility studies and consultancy support
Grants of up to £3,000 are available towards the cost of consultancy work looking at the possibility of utilising microelectronics in their products or production processes

Development
The development costs to commercial production of new or significantly improved products may be eligible for a grant of up to $33\frac{1}{3}$% of qualifying costs (e.g. hardware and software trial installations, licensing and consultancy fees), or in exceptional cases, a shared-cost contract of up to 50%.
To be eligible for any of the above, the company must be able to show that:

— it is viable, and has the technical and financial capability to carry the project through
— the project must have a good prospect of success, and improve the company's performance
— Additionality

The total qualifying costs must not exceed £500,000.
Department of Industry, MAP Information Centre,
Electronics Applications Division
29 Bressenden Place
London SW1E 5DT
Tel: 01 213 5836

10. Flexible manufacturing systems
Flexible manufacturing is a system which combines micro-electronics and mechanical engineering to bring economics of scale to batch work. A central on-line computer controls machine tools and other work stations and other components and tooling whilst also providing monitoring and information control. This combination of flexibility and over all control makes possible the production of a wide range of products in small numbers.
Grants are available to companies operating within the UK and which come within Division 3 of the 1980 Standard Industrial Classification. Assistance is given on a selective basis and in assessing the projects the Department of Industry will take into consideration:
— the viability of the company and the project
— the degree of innovation in both the system and in the project's contribution to the whole manufacturing process
— whether the project introduces flexible manufacturing to a new sector of industry, or a new area of the country
— whether the project will act as a stimulus to the supply industry
— whether assistance would speed up the introduction of the project
Grants of 50% of professional consultancy fees are available up to a maximum of £50,000. The consultants must be approved by the Department of Industry.

Grants of up to $33\frac{1}{3}\%$ are available towards development and capital costs, minimum expenditure £200,000.

For further information contact:
Department of Industry
Mechanical and Engineering Division
Ashdown House
123 Victoria Street
London SW1E 6RB
Tel: 01 212 6515

11. Industrial robot support programme

All manufacturing companies are eligible for selective assistance, and in exceptional circumstances non-manufacturing operations may be given support in one of the following categories:

Consultancy support

50% of the cost of feasibility studies under-taken by independent consultants to establish whether robots can make an economic contribution to the product processes. The study may last up to 15 man days.

Application

The capital and development costs associated with installing an industrial robot may attract a grant of up to $33\frac{1}{3}\%$. The minimum project cost is £25,000, although smaller schemes may be considered.

Manufacture

A grant of up to $33\frac{1}{3}\%$ of qualifying costs is available to UK manufacturers of new industrial robots towards development and capital costs for projects involving design and development. The qualifying costs may include such things as the design and development of prototypes, trials modifications and launching. Assistance is available for placing the newly designed robots with users for evaluation on the same basis as under the Support For Innovation scheme.

Department of Industry
Mechanical and Electrical Engineering Division
Room 420
Ashdown House
123 Victoria Street
London SW1E 6RB
Tel: 01 212 0724

12. Fibre optics and opto-electronics scheme
All firms involved in the design, development and application of products and processes related to optical fibres, opto-electronics, optical sensors and instruments required for these activities can apply for support under this scheme.

Development
A grant of 33⅓% is available towards the costs of research and development, similar to that available under Support for Innovation. A shared-cost contract of up to 50% may be offered in exceptional circumstances. The minimum qualifying cost must be £25,000.

Application
A grant of 33⅓% or a pre-production order is available for developing novel applications of fibre optic and opto-electronic technology. Criteria of eligibility are the same as under the Support for Innovation scheme.

Manufacture
Capital investment projects can attract a grant towards the cost of buildings, plant and equipment. The minimum project cost should normally be at least £500,000.
Applications for assistance must be received by 30 June 1986.

For further information contact:
Department of Industry
Electronics Applications Division
29 Bressenden Place
London SW1E 5DT
Tel: 01 213 5816

13. Biotechnology scheme
This scheme is aimed at promoting investment in biotechnology research and development projects. The industries involved in this sector are food, agriculture, pharmaceuticals, chemicals, waste-treatment, mining, process plant and control equipment, scientific equipment and reagents, horticulture and oil.

Consultancy support
Feasibility studies into specific process and product developments, and markets, can attract a grant of up to 75% or projects costs (to a project limit of £10,000).
Strategic studies to assess the commercial opportunities and risks presented by biotechnology may be eligible for grants of up to 50%, maximum grant £25,000.

Innovation grants
A grant of up to $33\frac{1}{3}\%$ towards support for research and development of innovative projects and processes, including demonstration projects is available.
For further information contact:

Biotechnology Unit
Laboratory of the Government Chemist
Department of Industry
Cornwall House
Stamford Street
London SE1 9NQ
Tel: 928 7900 ext. 601/628

14. British technology group (BTG)
The British Technology Group combines the activities of the National Enterprise Board and the National Research Development Corporation, and its aim is to promote innovation and investment in industry.
The BTG can provide finance for technical innovation in a variety of forms:

Joint venture finance
The BTG will provide 50% of the total cash flow required for a specific project, recoverable by a percentage levy on sales of the resulting product or process.

Loan finance and equity
Where a company is set up in order to exploit a new invention, or technical innovation, loan finance and equity may be provided on venture capital terms.

Small company innovation fund (SCIF)
The Small Companies Division of the Group has set up a fund specifically designed to assist small innovative businesses to develop new products and processes.
Packages are tailored to the requirements of the individual applicants, and can combine two or more forms of finance-loans, preference shares and equity funding.
For further details on the above contact:

British Technology Group
101 Newington Causeway
London SE1 6BU
Tel: 01 403 6666

National selective assistance
Selective assistance under Section 8 of the industry Industrial Development Act 1982 is available throughout the U.K. (including the assisted areas) for major projects which are in the National interest. Assisted projects should normally involve new investment of at least £500,000 including working capital and ancillary costs associated with the new project. Assistance is provided on a selective basis and directed towards manufacturing industry. Consideration will be given for commercially viable projects (projects where there is a genuine choice of international location) which will lead to substantial improvements in performance usually productivity although other improvements such as quality or reliability of products will be considered — which will lead to the introduction of new products to the business — the project must produce a substantial net contribution to U.K. output or by way of import substitution.
As with selective assistance under section 7 of the Industrial Development Act discussed earlier in this chapter, aid will only be given for projects that would not go ahead as proposed without aid. This means there must be a genuine and significant enhancement of the project as a result of the assistance (additionality).
The assistance provided will be *negotiated* as the minimum necessary to allow the project to succeed. Usually it will be provided in the form of cash grant payable over the length of the project and payment made in installments. Contact:

The Industrial Development Unit,
Department of Industry,
66/74 Victoria Street,
London, SW1E 6SJ
Telephone: 01 212 4150

or The Scottish Economic Planning Department
or Welsh Office Industry Department.

Coal firing schemes
This scheme is to encourage commercial undertakings in the manufacturing industry, agriculture and certain service industries (excluding banking and insurance) to switch industrial equipment from oil and/or gas to coal firing. Assistance is available in the U.K. and is discretionary in that the soundness of the proposal plus the additionality criteria be taken into account. The assistance will be by way of a capital grant of up to 25% of the net eligible cost of the project (i.e. net of VAT and of any applicable regional development grant or European Community grant). The mininum expenditure limit is £15,000 and there is no maximum.

ECSC loans have been made available to cover 50% of the cost of the conversion scheme which is eligible for the above mentioned grant. The loans will only be for 8 years with a 4 year grace period on the repayment of capital. Exchange risk guarantee scheme cover is also available. The borrowing limits for ECSC loans are minimum £7,500 maximum £2 million pounds. For further information contact:

Department of Industry,
Coal Firing Unit,
South East Regional Office,
375 Kensington High Street,
London W14 8QH
Telephone: 01 603 2060

For applicants in Northern Ireland contact:
Department of Economic Development,
Energy Division,
Massey Avenue,
Belfast.
Scotland — Scottish Economic Planning Department
Wales — The Industrial Division of the Welsh Department of Industry.

Small engineering firms investment scheme

This scheme was introduced on the 30th March, 1982 to make available to engineering firms employing less than 200 people a third of the cost investment of certain types of advanced capital equipment. The initial scheme was very successful in that the allocation of funds was quickly taken up and in March 1983 a further £100 million pounds was allocated to this scheme over the next three years.
For further information contact:
The Department of Industry, Regional Offices.

Small firms service

The Small Firms service is designed to help owners and managers of small businesses with their plans and problems. It acts as an advisory service to those people thinking of starting their own business as well as to people who are currently in business.
In general small firms can be considered for help and the criteria is employing less than 200 persons. Information is free but for further counselling after the initial free meeting a modest fee is charged for each subsequent session. A wide range of business information and management advice can be given and for help you should contact your Regional Small Firms Centre, dial 100 and ask the operator for Freefone 2444.

BUSINESS EXPANSION SCHEME

The aim of this scheme is to encourage investment in new, small business by means of income tax incentives. The incentives are given to outside investors, rather than a person putting money into his or her own business.

The scheme includes almost all manufacturing, construction and service industries, including the retail and wholesale trades, the main exclusions being those companies involved in financial services, overseas companies, and subsidiaries.

The normal minimum investment by any investor in any one company is £500, and to qualify for full relief the capital must be invested for a period of at least 5 years. Relief is given at the investor's top rate of tax. (Each individual's maximum investments now = £40000).

Under the terms of the scheme you can not qualify for relief if you are closely connected with the company i.e. you own more than 30% of the ordinary shares, you are a paid director, you are a partner or employee. For these purposes you count in with your own shares and interests those of your husband or wife, grandparents, parents, children or grandchildren. You can qualify for relief if you invest in a company controlled by your sister or brother, nephew or neice, or more distant relatives.

These are only very broad outlines of the scheme, and before investing you should obtain appropriate professional advice to ensure that you are eligible to benefit.

For further information contact:
Board of Inland Revenue
Press Office
Somerset House
Strand
London WC2R 1LB

Loan guarantees for small businesses

Under this scheme small businesses may be eligible for a loan guarantee by the Secretary of State for Industry.

Sole traders, partnerships, cooperatives and limited companies either already trading or starting up can apply to one of the financial institutions participating in the scheme for a loan of up to £75,000. The application must be for new or additional borrowings for capital spending or working capital. The lender must be satisfied that the project is a viable one, and that funds are not available from conventional sources.

Security will be required, but it will be based on the business assets rather than personal security.

The loans are usually repayable over a period of 2–7 years by quarterly or monthly instalments, and capital repayments can be deferred for up to 2 years.
The government guarantees 80% of the loan, for which a premium of 3% on the guaranteed amount outstanding is charged. Interest rates are set by the lender, and the effect of the 3% premium is to add 2.4% to that rate (i.e. 80% of 3%).
Most goods and services are covered by the scheme, but there are a few exclusions:
— Agriculture and Horticulture
— Banking and Finance
— Commission Agents
— Education
— Forestry
— House and Estate Agents
— Insurance Services
— Medical Health Services
— Veterinary Services
— Nightclubs and Licensed Clubs
— Postal Services
— Telecommunications
— Recreational and Cultural Service
— Tied Public Houses and Bars
— Travel Agents
Applications for the Loan Guarantee Scheme should be made to your bankers.
For further information contact:

Department of Industry
Loan Guarantee Unit
Room 212
Ashdown House
123 Victoria Street
London
SW1E 6RB
Tel: 01 212 8916

The enterprise allowance
Often people starting up in business, who have previously been unemployed, lose their regular income in the form of unemployment or supplementary benefit. An allowance of £40 per week for up to one year can be paid to individuals who:
— are between 18 and pensionable age
— have been unemployed or under notice of redundancy for 13 weeks
— have been receiving supplementary or unemployment benefit

— can show that they have £1,000 which they intend to invest in a new business
— will be working full time in the new business

Until recently this scheme has been operated in a few pilot areas, it has now been extended to cover the whole country and will run until 31 March 1984.
For further information contact your local Jobcentre.

British technology group (BTG)
In addition to the other assistance which it provides (see page 000), the BTG's Small Business Division offers two schemes for financing small firms with growth potential:
Oakwood Loan Finance Ltd.
Standardised 5 year loans are available to limited companies in England who need funds for growth but can not provide the normal security. Loans are available up to a maximum of £50,000, at an interest rate of 2% above base rate. Capital repayments commence at the beginning of the fourth year of the loan period. Oakwood will normally seek a warrant from the company entitling it to subscribe to no more than 20% of the equity at a future date, the company will be able to buy back the warrant at the end of the loan period according to a predetermined formula.

Small Company innovation fund (SCIF)
Individually designed packages can be provided for small innovative companies. Where equity is part of the package SCIF will take only a minority stake and will not involve itself in the routine running of the company.
For further details contact:

Small Companies Division
British Technology Group
101 Newington Causeway
London SE1 6BU
Tel: 01 403 6666

Industrial and commercial finance corporation
The ICFC is part of the Finance for Industry Group which is owned by the major Scottish and English clearing banks, and the Bank of England. It is an independent company which raises its funds from the private sector, and lends to small and medium sized companies throughout the UK, and is one of the largest sources of finance for these businesses.
ICFC provides finance in a variety of forms, and tailors every package to meet the individual requirements of the applicants, it can provide loans, subscribe for or purchase shares, hire purchase, leasing and guarantees.

It offers finance for business start-ups as well as expansion projects, and may seek a minority share in the equity of a new company (although it rarely interferes in the running of the business).
Loan repayments are normally between 5 and 20 years at competitive rates of interest. The rate is fixed at the beginning of the loan, and interest charged on the outstanding balance.
The ICFC is an agent for the European Investment Bank and European Commission, and the European Coal and Steel Community and is able to make funds available to small firms under the relevant schemes. The amounts available range from £15,000 to £250,000 and can represent up to 50% of the capital expenditure on any project. To qualify companies must be in the manufacturing, selected service or tourist industries. Within the Assisted Areas, the upper limit for loans is £2m.
The European loans can be given at an interest rate below the market rate, and capital repayments may be deferred for the first two years.
Enquiries should be addressed to any of ICFC's Area Offices, or:

ICFC
91 Waterloo Road
London SE1 8XP
Tel: 01 928 7822

Industrial common ownership movement

The Industrial Common Ownership Movement offers finance to new and expanding worker cooperatives through the Industrial Common Ownership Finance Ltd.
There are no set limits for the loans, but loans of less than £1,000 are not usually given, and the average range is £5,000 to £15,000. Loans are made for periods of up to 5 years at slightly less than commercial rates, and security is normally required.

Industrial Common Ownership Finance Ltd.
4 St. Giles Street
Northampton NN1 1AA
Tel: 0604 37563

(1) Standard Industrial Classifications — 1980

Division 0 Agriculture, Forestry and Fishing

01 Agriculture and Horticulture
02 Forestry
03 Fishing

Division 1 Energy and Water Supply Industries

11 Coal Extraction and Manufacturing of Solid Fuels
12 Coke Ovens
13 Extraction of Mineral Oil and Natural Gas
14 Mineral Oil Processing
15 Nuclear Fuel Production
16 Production and Distribution of Electricity, Gas and Other Forms of Energy
17 Water Supply Industry

Division 2 Extraction of Minerals and Ores other than Fuels; Manufacture of Metals, Mineral Products and Chemicals

21 Extraction and Preparation of Metalliferous Ores
22 Metal Manufacture
23 Extraction of Minerals, not elsewhere specified
24 Manufacture of Non-Metallic Mineral Products
25 Chemical Industry
26 Production of Man-Made Fibres

Division 3 Metal Goods, Engineering and Vehicle Industries

31 Manufacture of Metal Goods not elsewhere specified
32 Mechanical Engineering
33 Manufacture of Office Machinery, Data Processing Equipment
34 Electrical and Electronic Engineering
35 Manufacture of Motor Vehicles and Parts thereof
36 Manufacture of other Transport Equipment
37 Instrument Engineering

Division 4 Other Manufacturing Industries

41/42 Food Drink and Tobacco Manufacturing Industries
43 Textile Industry
44 Manufacture of Leather and Leather Goods
45 Footwear and Clothing Industries
46 Timber and Wooden Furniture Industries
47 Manufacture of Paper and Paper Products, Printing and Publishing
48 Processing of Rubber and Plastics
49 Other Manufacturing Industries

Division 5 Construction

50 Construction

Division 6 Distribution, Hotels and Catering; Repairs

61 Wholesale Distribution (except dealing in Scrap and Waste Materials)
62 Dealing in Scrap and Waste Materials
63 Commission Agents

64/65
Retail Distribution
66 Hotels and Catering
67 Repair of Consumer Goods and Vehicles

Division 7 Transport and Communications

71 Railways
72 Other Inland Transport
73 Sea Transport
75 Air Transport
76 Supporting Services
77 Miscellaneous Transport Services and Storage not elsewhere specified
79 Postal Services and Telecommunications

Division 8 Banking, Finance, Insurance, Business Services and Leasing

81 Banking and Finance
82 Insurance, Except for Compulsory Social Security
83 Business Services
84 Renting of Movables
85 Owning and Dealing in Real Estate

Division 9 Other Services

91 Public Administration, National Defence and Compulsory Social Security
92 Sanitary Services
93 Education
94 Research and Development
95 Medical and Other Health Services: Veterinary Services
96 Other Services Provided to the General Public
97 Recreational Services and Other Cultural Services
98 Personal Services
99 Domestic Services
100 Diplomatic Representation, International Organizations. Allied Armed Forces.

(2) Standard Industrial Classifications — 1968
Main minimum list headings in orders II to XX
Order II Mining and Quarrying

101 Coal Mining
102 Stone and Slate Quarrying and Mining
103 Chalk, Clay, Sand, and Gravel Extraction
104 Petroleum and Natural Gas
109 Other Mining and Quarrying

Order III Food, Drink and Tobacco

211 Grain Milling
212 Bread and Flour Confectionery
213 Biscuits
214 Bacon Curing, Meat and Fish Products
215 Milk and Milk Products
216 Sugar
217 Cocoa, Chocolate and Sugar Confectionery
218 Fruit and Vegetable Products
219 Animal and Poultry Foods
212 Vegetable and Animal Oils and Fats
229 Food Industries not elsewhere specified
231 Brewing and Malting
232 Soft Drinks
239 Other Drink Industries
240 Tobacco

Order IV Coal and Petroleum Products

261 Coke Ovens and Manufactured Fuel
262 Mineral Oil Refining
263 Lubricating Oils and Greases

Order V Chemicals and Allied Industries

271 General Chemicals
272 Pharmaceutical Chemicals and Preparations
273 Toilet Preparations
274 Paint
275 Soap and Detergents
276 Synthetic Resins and Plastics Materials and Synthetic Rubber
277 Dyestuffs and Pigments
278 Fertilizers
279 Other Chemical Industries

Order VI Metal Manufacture

311 Iron and Steel (General)
312 Steel Tubes
313 Iron Castings, etc
321 Aluminium and Aluminium Alloys
322 Copper, Brass and Other Copper Alloys
323 Other Base Metals

Order VII Mechanical Engineering

331 Agricultural Machinery (except tractors)
332 Metal-Working Machine Tools
333 Pumps, Valves and Compressors
334 Industrial Engines
335 Textile Machinery and Accessories
336 Construction and Earth-Moving Equipment
337 Mechanical and Handling Equipment
338 Office Machinery
339 Other Machinery
341 Industrial (including process) Plant and Steelwork
342 Ordnance and Small Arms
349 Other Mechanical Engineering not elsewhere specified

Order VIII Instrument Engineering

351 Photographic and Document Copying Equipment
352 Watches and Clocks
353 Surgical Instruments and Appliances
354 Scientific and Industrial Instruments and Systems

Order IX Electrical Engineering

361 Electrical Machinery
362 Insulated Wires and Cables
363 Telegraph and Telephone Apparatus and Equipment
364 Radio and Electronic Components
365 Broadcast Receiving and Sound Reproducing Equipment
366 Electronic Computers
367 Radio, Radar and Electronic Capital Goods
368 Electric Appliances Primarily for Domestic Use
369 Other Electrical Goods

Order X Shipbuilding and Marine Engineering

370 Shipbuilding and Marine Engineering

Order XI Mechanical Engineering

380 Wheeled Tractor Manufacturing
381 Motor Vehicle Manufacturing
382 Motor Clyde, Tricycle and Pedal Cycle Manufacturing
383 Aerospace Equipment Manufacturing and Repairing
384 Locomotives and Railway Track Equipment
385 Railway Carriages and Wagons and Trams

Order XII Metal Goods Not Elsewhere Specified

390 Engineers' Small Tools and Gauges
391 Hand Tools and Implements
392 Cutlery, Spoons, Forks, and Plated Tableware, etc.
393 Bolts, Nuts, Screws, Rivets, etc.
394 Wire and Wire Manufactures
395 Cans and Metal Boxes
396 Jewellery and Precious Metals
399 Metal Industries not elsewhere specified

Order XIII Textiles

411 Production of Man-Made Fibres
412 Spinning and Doubling on the Cotton and Flax Systems
413 Weaving of Cotton, Linen and Man-Made Fibres
414 Woollen and Worsted
415 Jute
416 Rope, Twine and Net
417 Hosiery and Other Knitted Goods
418 Lace
419 Carpets
421 Narrow Fabrics (not more than 30 cm wide)
422 Made-Up Textiles
423 Textile Finishing
429 Other Textile Industries

Order XIV Leather, Leather Goods and Fur

431 Leather (Training and Dressing) and Fellmongery
432 Leather Goods
433 Fur

Order XV Clothing and Footwear

441 Weatherproof Outerwear
442 Men's and Boys' Tailored Outerwear
443 Women's and Girls' Tailored Outerwear
444 Overalls and Men's Shirts, Underwear, etc
445 Dresses, Lingerie, Infants' Wear, etc
446 Hats, Caps and Millinery
449 Dress Industries not elsewhere specified
450 Footwear

Order XVI Bricks, Pottery, Glass, Cement, etc

461 Bricks, Fireclay and Refractory Goods
462 Pottery
463 Glass
464 Cement
469 Abrasives and Building Materials, etc, not elsewhere specified

Order XVII Timber, Furniture, etc
471 Timber
472 Furniture and Upholstery
473 Bedding, etc
474 Shop and Office Fitting
475 Wooden Containers and Baskets
479 Miscellanous Wood and Cork Manufactures

Order XVIII Paper, Printing and Publishing
481 Paper and Board
482 Packaging Products of Paper, Board and Associated Materials
483 Manufactured Stationery
484 Manufactures of Paper and Board not elsewhere specified
485 Printing, Publishing of Newspapers
486 Printing, Publishing of Periodicals
489 Other Printing, Publishing, Bookbinding, Engraving, etc

Order XIX Other Manufacturing Industries
491 Rubber
492 Linoleum, Plastic Floor-Covering, Leathercloth, etc
493 Brushes and Brooms
494 Toys, Games, Children's Carriages and Sports Equipment
495 Miscellaneous Stationers' Goods
496 Plastics Products not elsewhere specified
499 Miscellaneous Manufacturing Industries

Order XX Construction
500 Construction

REGIONAL DEVELOPMENT GRANTS OFFICES

Department of Industry, Kingsgate House, 66–74 Victoria Street, London SW1E 6SJ. Tel: 01 212 7676

Department of Industry, Regional Development Grants Office, Queensway House, West Precinct, Town Centre, Billingham, Cleveland TS23 2NF. Tel: 0642 553671

Department of Industry, Regional Development Grants Office, St Peter's House, Stanley Precinct, Bootle, Merseyside L20 3LZ. Tel: 051 922 4030

Department of Industry, Regional Development Grants Office, 24–26 Newport Road, Cardiff CF2 1SY. Tel: 0222 492611

Department of Industry, Regional Development Grants Office, Magnet House, 59 Waterloo Street, Glasgow G2 7BT. Tel: 041 221 9833

DEPARTMENT OF INDUSTRY OFFICES

England
Department of Industry, Kingsgate House, 66–74 Victoria Street, London SW1E 6SJ. Tel: 01 212 7676

North Eastern Region, Stanegate House, 2 Groat Market, Newcastle upon Tyne NE1 1YN. Tel: 0632 324722

North Western Region, Sunley Building, Piccadilly Plaza, Manchester M1 4BA. Tel: 061 236 2171

Merseyside Sub-Office, 1 Old Hall Street, Liverpool L3 9HJ. Tel: 051 236 5756

Yorkshire & Humberside Region, Priestley House, 1 Park Row, City Square, Leeds LS1 5LF. Tel: 0532 443171

Location and selective financial assistance enquiries:
South West Industrial Development Office, Phoenix House, Notte Street, Plymouth PL1 2HF. Tel: 0752 21891

Scotland
Locate in Scotland, Scottish Development Agency, 120 Bothwell Street, Glasgow G2 7JP. Tel: 041 248 2700

Wales
Welsh Office, Industry Department, New Crown Building, Cathays Park, Cardiff CF1 3NQ. Tel: 0222 825111

Northern Ireland Belfast
Industrial Development Board for Northern Ireland, IDB House, 64 Chichester Street, Belfast BT1 4JX. Tel: 0232 34488

West Midlands Region, Ladywood House, Stephenson Street, Birmingham B2 4DT. Tel: 021 632 4111

East Midlands Region, Severns House, 20 Middle Pavement, Nottingham NG1 7DW. Tel: 0602 56181

South Eastern Region, Charles House, 375 Kensington High Street, London W14 8QH. Tel: 01 603 2060

South West Region, The Pithay, Bristol BS1 2PB. Tel: 0272 291071

North Wales District Office, Government Buildings, Dinerth Road, Colwyn Bay, Clwyd LL28 4UL. Tel: 0492 44261

London
Industrial Development Board for Northern Ireland, Ulster Office, 11 Berkeley Street, London W1X 6BU. Tel. 01 493 0601

DEPARTMENT OF EMPLOYMENT OFFICES

Northern Regional Office, Wellbar House, Gallowgate, Newcastle upon Tyne NE1 4TP. Tel: 0632 27575

Yorkshire and Humberside Regional Office, City House, New Station Street, Leeds LS1 4JH. Tel: 0532 38232

London and South-East Regional Office, Hanway House, 27–31 Red Lion Square, London WC1R 4NH. Tel: 01-405 8454

South West Regional Office, The Pithay, Bristol BS1 2NQ. Tel: 0272 291071

Midlands Regional Office, 2 Duchess Place, Hagley Road, Birmingham B16 8NS. Tel: 021 455 7111

North West Regional Office, Sunley Building, Piccadilly Plaza, Manchester M60 7JS. Tel: 061 832 9111

Office for Scotland, Pentland House, 47 Robbs Loan, Edinburgh EH1 1UE. Tel: 031 443 8731

Office for Wales, Companies House, Crown Way, Maindy, Cardiff CF4 3UW. Tel. 0222 388588

BRITISH TECHNOLOGY GROUP — REGIONAL OFFICES

Centro House, 3 Cloth Market, Newcastle upon Tyne NE1 1EH. Tel: 0632 327068

Century House, Floor 6, 7 Tib Lane, Manchester M2 4JX. Tel: 061 834 6406

9 Bond Court, Leeds LS1 2SN. Tel: 0532 459858

Richmond House, 1 Rumford Place, Liverpool L3 9QY. Tel: 051 227 1366

NRDC Office in Scotland, 87 St. Vincent Street, Glasgow G2 5TF. Tel: 041 221 1820

Phoenix House, Notte Street, Plymouth PL1 2HS. Tel: 0752 665262

REGIONAL OFFICES OF ENGLISH INDUSTRIAL ESTATES

Gateshead
(covering Northumberland, Tyne & Wear), Methven House, Kingsway, Team Valley, Gateshead, Tyne and Wear NE11 0LN. Tel: 0632 874711

Thornaby
(covering Cleveland, Durham and North Yorkshire), Forster House, Allensway, Thornaby-on-Tees, Cleveland TS17 9HA. Tel: 0642 765911

Workington
(covering Cumbria), Salterbeck Industrial Estate, Workington, Cumbria CA14 5DX. Tel: 0946 830469

Liverpool
(covering North West and West Midlands), Sandon House, 157 Regent Road, Liverpool L5 9TF. Tel: 051 933 2020

Doncaster
(covering Yorkshire & Humberside, East Midlands and East Anglia), Hallgate House, 19 Hallgate, Doncaster, South Yorkshire DN1 3NN. Tel: 0302 66865

Bodmin
(covering South West and South of England), 53 Fore Street, Bodmin, Cornwall PL31 2JB. Tel: 0208 3631/4

INDUSTRIAL AND COMMERCIAL FINANCE CORPORATION LIMITED

London
91 Waterloo Road, London SE1 8XP. Tel: 01-928 7822

Area Offices also at

Aberdeen
Birmingham
Brighton
Bristol
Cambridge
Cardiff
Edinburgh
Glasgow
Leeds
Leicester
Liverpool
Manchester
Newcastle
Nottingham
Reading
Sheffield
Southampton

5. A Cautionary Tale

I mentioned earlier the Small Business Loan Guarantee Scheme and how it has helped many small firms. The amount to 31.3.83 currently out on loan is £312.6 million and this is split between 9396 businesses.

In November 1982 Robson Rhodes — Chartered Accountants reported on the circumstances giving rise to the first 50 claims made on the Department of Industry in respect of failed businesses. Robson Rhodes were appointed by the Secretary of State for Industry to report on a range of matters as required by the Department of Industry Economics Division.

Robson Rhodes were able to study 48 of the 50 cases, as in 2 cases it proved impossible to gain access to the necessary information file. It's only fair to point out that the survey studied only failures and not successes — it would need a much wider survey before comment could be made on the Loan Guarantee Scheme as a whole. (To date 560 guarantees have been called on.)

However, I think it's worth pulling out some of the main points as there are some revealing comments on why businesses failed.

Let's start by explaining the scheme.

The small business loan guarantee scheme (SBLGS)

Introduction

Under arrangements announced by the Chancellor of the Exchequer on 10 March, 1981, small businesses in England, Scotland and Wales may be eligible for a loan guarantee by the Secretary of State for Trade and Industry under Section 8 of the Industry Act 1972. In suitable cases, the Secretary of State will be prepared to guarantee repayment of 80% of medium-term loans (not overdrafts) made by the English and Scottish Clearing Banks and ICFC to eligible small businesses for business purposes only. In consideration for this guarantee the Department of Industry will charge a commercial premium payable quarterly.

Eligibility

Applications for loans under the scheme, which should be made to one of the participating financial institutions, may be from sole traders, partnerships, co-operatives or limited companies. They may be already trading or they may be starting in business. There is no formal limitation based on numbers employed, turnover, assets etc., but applications will not be considered from large businesses or their subsidiaries. Most sectors of the economy involving tradeable goods and services are covered but there are some areas which are excluded.

Excluded activities

Agriculture and horticulture
Banking and finance and associated services
Commission agents
(units primarily engaged in acting as intermediaries between buyer and seller and in carrying out transactions for the principal's account)
Education
(including driving and flying schools providing training for non-commercial purposes)
Forestry
(except tree harvesting and saw milling)
House and estate agents
Insurance and associates services
Medical and health services, veterinary services
Nightclubs and licensed clubs
Owning and dealing in real estate
Postal services and telecommunications
Public administration, national defence and compulsory social security
Railways
Recreational services and other cultural services.
Tied public houses and bars.
Travel agents.

Further clarification may be obtained from the Department of Industry's Loan Guarantee Unit.

Amount and duration of loans

Guaranteed loans may be for amounts of up to £75,000 repayable over periods of between two and seven years.

Interest rate and other bank charges

The interest rate appropriate to individual guarantee loans will be decided by the lender, who will also charge an arrangement fee in accordance with his usual practice. The Government's guarantee will reduce the risk borne by the lender, who will take this into account when deciding the interest rate appropriate to individual cases.

Premiums
The Department of Industry will charge a premium, usually 3% of the guaranteed amount (i.e. 80% of the loan). The premium will reduce as the loan is repaid. Arrangements will be made for the premium to be paid quarterly in advance by direct debit.

Security
Applicants must be prepared to pledge all available assets used, or available for use, in connection with the business as security for guaranteed loans. This will not necessarily exclude from the scheme cases where none are available.

Appraisal of applications
The primary appraisal of applications for guaranteed loans will be carried out by the lender, who must be satisfied that the proposition is viable, and is not one that he can sanction without the guarantee, before he can forward an application to the Department of Industry.

Participating financial institutions
Barclays Bank Limited
Lloyds Bank Limited
Midland Bank Limited
National Westminster Bank Limited
Williams and Glyn's Bank Limited
Bank of Scotland
Royal Bank of Scotland Limited
Clydesdale Bank Limited
Industrial and Commercial Finance Corporation Limited
Example documents for these schemes are shown on the following pages.

The objectives of the scheme
1. The Scheme, perhaps deliberately, was loosely formulated by the Government and intended to be worked out in detail with the banks. It was impossible to determine beforehand whether or not such a Scheme was required to fill a gap in the market for small business funds. Following a series of discussions with the banks, the Government decided to introduce a pilot scheme on a trial basis for three years.
2. What was envisaged was a Scheme which would facilitate an increase in the number of small business start-ups and expansions.
3. This would be done by encouraging the banks to make advances to potential borrowers who put forward propositions which, although viable, by their nature or due to the borrowers' lack of available security, fell outside the scope of normal banking practice. For instance, where a borrower was unable to pledge adequate personal

Small Firms Loan Guarantee Scheme

PROPOSAL AND GUARANTEE

To: THE SECRETARY OF STATE FOR INDUSTRY

Pursuant to an application made by the applicant named below as the borrower ("the Borrower") the Bank named below as lender ("the Bank") is willing, subject to the issue by the Secretary of State for Industry ("the Secretary of State") of a guarantee under Section 8 of the Industry Act 1972 in the form of that appearing overleaf, to offer to the Borrower a loan facility on the terms set out below and in the Bank's usual form of Small Firms Loan Guarantee Scheme facility letter.

Lender

Name ....

Address ....

....

....

....

The Facility

Amount £..............................

Term .... years

Arrangement Fee

.... % of the Facility payable on acceptance.

Date of Application ..../.............../...............

Borrower

Name ....

Business Address ....

....

....

Registered Office *(if different from above)*

....

....

....

Purpose of Facility

....

....

....

....

Security *Only Permitted Security should be specified*

A B *Enter a tick in Box A if the security is already held. Enter a tick in Box B where the security is to be taken.*

☐ ☐ *1. A Floating Charge / an Unlimited Debenture / a Debenture* in the Bank's standard form over the Borrower's undertaking and assets.

☐ ☐ *2. Legal Charge(s) in the Bank's standard form over the property described below

Full description of property ....

....

....

....

....

....

Name and address of beneficial owner *(if other than the Borrower)*

....

....

....

....

....

☐ ☐ *3. Other form(s) of security *(give details)* ....

....

....

....

....

....

*delete as appropriate

Repayment

Repayment to be made in .... equal monthly / quarterly* instalments commencing .... months after the loan is drawn down

**delete as appropriate*

Interest

Interest Rate

% per annum ("the Margin") over the Bank's Base Rate but with a minimum of % per annum ("the Minimum Rate")

Interest Payment Dates

Interest will be payable quarterly on the Bank's usual charging dates.

Bank's Proposal

We confirm that:

(a) we would not consider it prudent for us to offer to the Borrower a loan facility identical in terms to the proposed facility but without the benefit of a guarantee of the Secretary of State upon the terms set out overleaf; and

(b) we would be prepared to make available the proposed facility with the benefit of such a guarantee.

Signed ....

for and on behalf of the Bank

Date ..../.............../...............

Existing Facilities

Type	*Existing Limit (£)*	*New Limit (£) (if proposal accepted)*
Overdraft		
Term Loans		
....		
....		
Other Liabilities		
....		
....		

N.B. *List all existing facilities*

Distribution

	To be retained by	*After receipt from*
First Copy (White)	Issuing Branch	Department of Industry
Second Copy (Blue)	Department of Industry	Corporate Business Dept.
Third Copy (Green)	Corporate Business Dept.	Local Head Office
Fourth Copy (Red)	Local Head Office	Issuing Branch
Fifth Copy (White)	Issuing Branch	

Guarantee

The Secretary of State hereby issues a guarantee upon the terms set out overleaf; the Guarantee Premium shall be payable at the rate of % per annum.

Signed ....

for and on behalf of the Secretary of State for Industry

Date ..../.............../...............

B 6/81 (England and Wales)

Small Firms Loan Guarantee Scheme
APPLICATION FORM

Name of Applicant ....
(Insert Full Name)

(Before completing this form please read carefully the notes on completion set out on the back)

Section A

To: ....
(Insert Name of Bank)

....
(Insert Name of Branch and its Sorting Code)

and

THE SECRETARY OF STATE FOR INDUSTRY

The Applicant named above requests (a) from the Bank ("the Bank") named above a loan facility pursuant to the Small Firms Loan Guarantee Scheme and (b) from the Secretary of State for Industry ("the Secretary of State") a guarantee under Section 8 of the Industry Act 1972 in favour of the Bank in respect of 80% of the Applicant's obligations under the facility

The amount and term of the loan requested by the Applicant are the following:

AMOUNT £ .... TERM .... Years
(not to exceed £75,000) *(to be between 2 and 7 years)*

The Applicant should note that if a loan facility is made available pursuant to this Application:

- a premium on the guaranteed portion of the facility will be payable quarterly in advance to the Secretary of State
- an Arrangement Fee of up to 1% of the facility will be payable to the Bank
- interest will be payable at an agreed margin over the Bank's Base Rate (a minimum rate may be specified)
- the Applicant may be required to provide security over assets used or available for use in connection with the applicant's business

The terms generally applicable to Scheme facilities are described in the Department of Industry's brochure

Section B

1. Business Address

....

....

....

2. Registered Office *(if applicable)*

....

....

....

3. Names of Partners / Directors / Committee Members *(if applicable)*

....

....

....

....

....

4. Main Activities

....

....

....

Number of Employees ....

Is the Facility for a new business? Yes / No *(delete as applicable)*

Trading Names ....

....

....

....

5. Legal Status

Sole Trader ☐ Partnership ☐ Limited Company ☐
Unlimited Company ☐ Industrial and Provident Society ☐
(Place a tick in the appropriate box)

6. Names of Shareholders / Members *(if applicable)*

....

....

....

....

....

....

....

....

7. Financial Information

The Applicant should submit with this Application

- a copy of its latest Audited Accounts and Management Accounts
- cash flow projections for the period of 12 months from the date of this Application
- a statement giving details of all its existing loan and bank facilities (including loans under the Small Firms Loan Guarantee Scheme) and any security given for those loans and facilities
- a detailed description of how the facility is to be used

Declarations

1. The Applicant warrants that the information given in this Application and any documents submitted herewith is true, complete and accurate in all respects and that the Applicant is not aware of any facts or circumstances not disclosed herein or therein which might, if disclosed, adversely affect the decision of a person considering whether or not to provide finance to the Applicant

2. The Applicant hereby authorises each of the Bank and the Secretary of State (a) to make such enquiries and take up such references in relation to this Application as either may consider appropriate and (b) to disclose to the other any information it may now or at any time hereafter have or acquire in connection with the Applicant whether before or after the entering into of any facility or the issue of any guarantee pursuant hereto

Signed by ....
on behalf of the Applicant

Date ..../........../..........

Names and Addresses of Witnesses *(Two witnesses are required in Scotland)*

Name ....
Address ....
....

Name ....
Address ....
....

security and where a risky but potentially viable project had no previous track record on which the lender could rely.

4. It was a condition of the Scheme that the banks should not seek personal guarantees from the owners of the business as security. Concomitantly, the Government's guarantee would be conditional upon the borrower pledging all available business assets.
5. Because the lending was to be marginal, the interest and premium were intended to be relatively expensive. This would ensure that the recipient would not receive a cost advantage over the bank's other borrowers. The scheme would thus act as a scheme of last resort.
6. The banks are required to certify that in the absence of the Scheme they would not have been prepared to make the proposed facility available.
7. The mechanics and administration of the Scheme, and the order of the application of money recovered on the discontinuance of the business, were settled by negotiation. The requirement for the borrower to draw the full amount of the loan in one lump sum within sixty days of the offer being made was subsequently modified to allow the drawdown to take place in up to four tranches of not less than 25% each.
8. The bank's assessment of the viability of the project, was more difficult to regulate. An assessment of viability was assumed to be a fundamental part of normal banking practice to be left to the discretion of the banks. The Government did not stipulate any criteria for viability.

The banks actioning of the scheme

1. As there was no authoritative publication of the 'rules' of the Scheme the banks were left to achieve the objectives. The eventual use of the scheme was dependent on bank managers and sanctioning officials in the regional offices of the banks.
2. Banks gave the Scheme their full support.
3. The primary objective was proposals should not be 'turned aside merely because the business was over-geared or this meant that the banks would be lending in some cases in a new experience.'
4. The banks do not appear to have issued any new instructions regarding appraisal procedures and the assessment of viability.
5. If a proposition was viable to bankers then they would be expected to lend via their own schemes. If not possible then consideration within the Scheme.
6. As with any new scheme the response appears to have been varied: some lenders were more cautious than others.
7. In some parts of the country some banks were more active than others in using the Scheme. The influence on lending under the Scheme rests with individual branch managers and the regional sanctioning officials.

8. Some bank managers have made it clear that there was strong encouragement to use the Scheme. One institution was specifically asked to use the Scheme on an experimental basis.

The failures studied

Table 1 analyses the 48 failures, between new and existing businesses, between start-ups, buy-outs, lending for expansion or to businesses in urgent need. Those existing businesses which were in urgent need are classified as being 'in distress'. The statistics indicate that in failures two-thirds of the loans were to existing businesses. Table 2 further elaborates, highlighting the fact that half the businesses defined as 'existing' had been in existence less than 12 months prior to the application for a Scheme loan.

Table 1
Analysis of failures between new and existing businesse

New business:		
Start-up	11	22.9%
Buy-out	5	10.4%
	16	33.3%
Existing businesses:		
Expansion	14	29.2%
Urgent need ('in distress')	18	37.5%
	32	66.7%
	48	

Table 2
Duration of existing business before application to LGS

Up to:		
6 months	8	
12 months	8	
	16	50%
2 years	7	
3 years	4	
More than 3 years	5	
	32	
Minimum	6 weeks	
Maximum	12 years	

62% of the businesses failed within six months of receiving the Scheme loan. Small businesses often succeed or fail in what they are trying to do in a very short time.

— The shortest period of life was in fact a matter of days.
— The loan failures varied between £5 000 and £75 000.
— The average loan amount was £30 270 and the 50 failures totalled £1.5m approximately.

Table 3
Activity analysis

		New	*Existing*	*Total*	
1.	Manufacturing				
	General	0	1	1	
	Capital goods	0	6	6	
	Household goods	4	10	14	
	Food	0	0	0	
	Processing	2	0	2	
	Packaging products	0	3	3	
		6	20	26	54.2%
2.	Construction	1	0	1	
3.	Dealers, merchants and distributors	0	1	1	
4.	Printing and publishing	5	0	5	
5.	Retailing	2	3	5	
6.	Industrial services	0	4	4	
7.	General services, maintenance	0	2	2	
8.	Office services	1	0	1	
9.	House and personal services	1	2	3	
	Totals	16	32	48	

This table shows 54.2% failures were in manufacturing or hoping to manufacture! You can draw your own conclusions from this.

Reasons for failure

1. Little evidence of responsible research into the market, how the business would operate, business control, the ability of management to measure its performance against forecast. In general, the presentation to banks lacked a link to the real way in which a business would be operated.
2. Lack of simple management information systems and how to analyse the crucial factors of a business and their inter-dependent behaviour.

Table 4
Reasons for failure

	Total
Market for product not as envisaged:	
— Forecasts unrealistic	3
— Forecasts optimistic but possible	5
— Market decline	4
	12
Reasonable market, but poor management	
— Personal problems*	8
— Poor management*	5
— Lack of financial control	3
— Poor marketing	4
— Business neglected	1
	21
— Production problems	7
— Competition	4
— Deception	2
— Loss of major customer	1
— Overtrading	1
	15
	48

*These two overlap

Its interesting to note from Table 4 that poor management was the cause of most failures. Also production problems and forecasts are both notable sectors.
Robson Rhodes looked to four basic business skills when assessing each case — marketing, production, finance and purchasing — and invariably, management was deficient in one or more of these skills.

Management advice

It is always worth remembering that you *can* talk your business plan through with someone else e.g. your accountant; the Bank Manager or your local Small Firms Information Centre (details of these are given in Chapter 6).
However, in the failure survey, in an overwhelming number of cases no practical management advice was taken from outsiders. See Table 5.

Table 5
Was practical management advice taken from outsiders?

	Total
Bank	3
Accountant	6
Financial institution	1
Non-executive board member	2
Someone else	4
	16
No-one	36
	52

The table shows 36 (70%) of failures took no advice at all!
What sort of advice should you seek?
- — how to market
- — how to assess the potential market
- — assessing your gross profit and understanding costs
- — the financial *structure* of your business

Break-even levels

The survey revealed that a material number of businesses had such a high break-even level that the forecast results would be virtually impossible to achieve.

Table 6
% of sales forecasts required to break-even

	Total
Up to 50%	3
50% to 60%	1
60% to 70%	6
	10
70% to 80%	3
80% to 90%	10
90% to 100%	5
Over 100%	2
	30
Details not known	18
	48

This table shows 20% of businesses had a reasonable level to break-even (up to 70%). However 37% of all cases the details were not known and as you can see a significant number required a high break-even level of sales. In the chapter on Financial Planning I explained how we can calculate quite simply the break-even point for your business. We also discussed other management information — profit budget, cost budget etc. The survey found little evidence of this type of information being prepared.

Table 7
Was management information prepared?

	Total	
Prepared		
Copies not supplied to bank	6	
Copies supplied to bank	13	
	19	
Not prepared	29	(60.4%)
	48	

It seems, therefore, that time taken to put in simple but sound bookkeeping routines and management information systems is time well spent.
Furthermore, monitoring of progress is vital and look at the survey results.

Table 8
Management information available for control of business

	Total	
Projection of income and expenditure		
Yes	28	
No	19	(40.4%)
Projection of cash flow		
Yes	47	(100%)
No	—	
Monthly statement of income		
Yes	6	
No	41	(87.2%)
Monthly cash flow		
Yes	2	
No	45	(95.7%)

The gearing of the failed business

We mentioned this earlier — in our Financial Planning Chapter. The significance of over borrowing is illustrated in the failures study.

Table 9
Initial capital gearing

	Total
Up to 1:1	3
1:1 to 2:1	7
2:1 to 3:1	3
3:1 to 5:1	4
5:1 to 10:1	2
10:1 to 20:1	1
Over 20:1	26
Information not available	2
	48

Over half the businesses had adverse gearing of over 20:1
Robson Rhodes concluded that it would seem probable that *any start-ups geared more than 5:1 should either benefit from some very unusual prospects or will need the closest attention in their early days.*
High break-even, high gearing and low margins make a business very vulnerable to any adversity.

Management experience

Again accepting the limitation of the survey its most revealing to look at the lack of experience in key areas:

In concluding this chapter I think it's important to state that although the Scheme has certainly helped many new businesses you should be careful to assess:

(i) Are your projections realistic and can you break-even at a comfortable level of output — say less than 70%?
(ii) Look at the gearing of your proposal and discuss this with your Bank Manager. Can you afford to service the debt structure?
(iii) Have you the necessary experience in key areas? If not seek advice!
(iv) Have you set up simple systems to carefully monitor progress — particularly in the early days of your business?

Table 10
Was there previous experience in the following areas?

	Total	
Marketing		
Yes	27	
No	21	(43.7%)
	48	
Production		
Yes	29	
No	11	(22.9%)
Information not available	1	
Not applicable	7	
	48	
Finance		
Yes	17	
No	29	(60.4%)
Information not available	2	
	48	
Purchasing		
Yes	20	
No	21	(43.7%)
Information not available	2	
Not applicable	5	
	48	

6. 88 Government Schemes to Help

In different sections of this book various government schemes have been mentioned. This chapter is a synopsis of all the 88 schemes available.

Finance

1. Loan guarantee scheme
A pilot loan scheme was introduced on 1 June 1981. It is designed to improve the flow of commercial funds to the entrepreneur with a viable business proposition which would not otherwise get financial backing. Individual term loans of up to £75,000 are available through participating financial institutions for periods of between 2 and 7 years. The Government guarantee will apply to 80% of each loan. The scheme is open to small business in most sectors of the economy.

2. The purchase of own shares legislation
The Companies Act 1981 has given power for limited companies to buy back their own shares.

3. British technology group small companies investment fund. (SCIF)
SCIF was formed in September 1980 to increase the availability of British Technology Group investment finance to innovative small companies. Most industrial funding has been in support of a specific innovatory project within a company but SCIF sets out to provide balance sheet funding for the overall operation of small companies whose business as a whole is innovative.

4. British technology group Oakwood Finance Ltd.
Oakwood offers loans of up to £50,000 to all sectors of industry but with special emphasis on high technology companies.

European loans

5. European investment bank: assisted areas
The Department of Industry (with Scottish and Welsh Offices and, later Northern Ireland Department of Economic Development) has since the beginning of 1978 operated an agency from the European Investment

Bank backed with exchange risk cover, designed to enable small to medium sized firms in the Assisted Areas and Northern Ireland to borrow sums of £15,000 — £4.25m.
Exchange risk agreements were signed in 1981 with Industrial and Commercial Finance Corporation (ICFC) and Midland Bank to assist them to make EIB foreign currency loans available to smaller firms in the Assisted Areas. National Westminster are now also in the scheme.

6. European investment bank: non-assisted areas
Since January 1982 European loans for small and medium-sized firms have been available outside the Assisted Areas through ICFC with the necessary exchange risk cover provided by the Government.

7. European coal and steel community (ECSC)
Loans are also available from the European coal and Steel Community (ECSC) for smaller manufacturing firms in coal and steel closure areas. Agreements providing exchange risk cover for these ECSC loans have been signed with ICFC, Barclays Bank, Midland Bank. Clydesdale Bank, National Westminster Bank, the Co-operative Bank, and both the Welsh and Scottish Development Agencies.

Tax incentives for the businessman

8. Corporation tax
A lower rate of 38% applies to profits of up to £100,000.

9. The VAT registration limit
VAT registration limit is £18,000.

10. Pre-registration VAT relief
Relief from VAT on services supplied before registration is now available to all traders.

11. Pre-trading income/corporation tax relief
Expenditure of a revenue nature incurred within three years prior to the commencement of trading is now allowed in computing the profits chargeable to tax when trade begins, provided that the expenditure would have been so allowable had it been incurred during a period of trading.

12. 3 Year carry-back of allowances
Unused first year capital allowances on plant and machinery may be set against trading profits made in the previous three years.

13. Pre-trading carryback of income tax losses
Tax losses are not uncommon in the early years of a business. Losses made in the first four years of trading may often be set against the proprietor's income for the previous three years — producing a repayment of tax paid before the business began.

14. Small workshops allowance
100% initial allowances on capital expenditure incurred on the construction of industrial premises of up to 1,250 sq ft until 26 March 1985.

15. Industrial buildings allowance: extension of part of the service sector
The definition of an industrial building for the purpose of these allowances has been widened to include buildings used for repair and servicing goods and those used for warehousing and storage by traders and wholesalers, where the goods involved are to be used for an industrial process. The Industrial Buildings Allowance also now applies to industrial buildings occupied under licence.

Tax incentives for the investor

16. Business expansion scheme
The Business Expansion Scheme is an entirely new tax incentive to attract individual investors to back unquoted trading companies. Where certain conditions are satisfied, an investor is able to obtain relief against income tax on up to £40,000 subscribed for shares issued in any one tax year.

17. Venture capital scheme
Losses on disposal of shares owned by individuals and investment companies in unquoted trading companies can now be set against income rather than capital gains.

18. Interest relief for investment in companies
Those who own more than 5% of 'close' companies, and managers of such companies, are entitled to tax relief if they pay interest on money borrowed to buy shares in their company.

19. Interest relief for investment in partnerships
A similar relief is available for those who invest money in industrial co-operatives and partnerships.

20. Capital gains retirement relief
Where an individual aged 60 years or more disposes (by sale or gift) of either (i) the whole or part of a business; or (ii) the shares in a family trading company of which he is a full time working director, then he or she is entitled to 'retirement relief'. (It is available separately to husbands and wives.) The maximum relief is £100,000 and is allowed against chargeable gains which would otherwise fall due from disposal of the assets. Maximum relief is available for an individual aged 65 or more and who has owned (or owned shares in) the business for ten years; the relief is progressively reduced if these conditions are not met.

21. Capital gains indexation
Annual revision of CGT thresholds in light of changes in the retail price index and principle of indexing (except for first 12 months) introduced for gains accruing after March 1982.

22. Capital transfer tax: ten year rule
Previous gifts are now ignored if made more than 10 years before a later gift or bequest. This means that lifetime gifts can often be made without increasing later tax liabilities, and this facilitates the transfer of business between generations.

22a. Capital transfer tax: business relief
For the purpose of charging Capital Transfer Tax, the value of a majority stake in an unquoted company is reduced by 50%. The value of a minority stake is reduced by 30%.

23. Purchase of own shares tax relaxation
To assist a number of small and family companies, the tax charge has been eased in certain cases where an unquoted trading company buys back shares for the benefit of the trade.

24. 1982 Share options legislation
Income tax payable by a director or employee on a gain arising from the exercise of an option to acquire shares may be paid by instalments over five years.

Support for innovation

25. New products and processes
A grant or shared cost contract available to firms towards the cost of developing new product or processes. It is also planned that, from the summer of 1983, there will be grants towards the cost of market

assessment studies, and towards the cost of production tooling, capital equipment and certain other pre-production costs.

26. Joint appraisal

The Joint Appraisal Scheme (JAS) was initially introduced for microelectronics applications, it is now open to anyone applying for Research and Development support. Under JAS, the Department of Industry's technical/commercial appraisal is made available to the financial institution nominated. Nineteen institutions are actively participating in the scheme — but applicants are not limited to these.

27. Computer-aided design/computer-aided manufacturing

A programme to promote and accelerate the acceptance and application of computer aids to design, draughting, planning, estimating and manufacture primarily in the mechanical and electrical engineering sectors of industry.

28. Computer-aided design/manufacture and test

A programme to encourage the use of computer aids in the design manufacture and testing of electronic systems.

29. Flexible manufacturing systems scheme

Selective financial assistance to encourage the use of systems which combine microelectronics and mechanical engineering to bring economies of scale to batch work by assisting with the costs of consultancy, development and capital equipment.

30. Fibre optics and opto-electronics scheme

Grants are available to encourage the development, launching and application of new products and processes relating to optical fibres, opto-electronics, optical sensors and instruments required for these activities.

31. Industrial robots support

Grants are available to encourage the increased use and manufacture of industrial robots.

32. Microelectronics application project

This scheme is designed to encourage UK manufacturing industry to make use of microelectronics technology. In addition to financial support for selected projects, the Department of Industry will also look at ways to assist with the cost of improving industrial awareness.

33. Microprocesor industry support programme

A grant or a shared cost contract is available to promote investment in the microelectronics component industry.

34. Software products scheme
A grant or a shared cost contract for service firms to encourage the development of software products or packages.

34a. Telecoms products scheme
Financial assistance is available to support the development and manufacture of new types of tele-communication equipment which are to be sold for attachment to British Telecom's network.

35. Purchase of pre-production models
The Department of Industry can purchase pre-production models (normally up to 4) of new or significantly improved equipment which the manufacture is having difficulty launching. The equipment is placed with potential users to evaluate before they decide whether to purchase, but should the equipment prove unsatisfactory the manufacturer must buy it back at the end of the trial period (normally a year) at an agreed price.

36. Research and development requirement boards
There are currently five Boards covering Mechanical and Electrical Engineering; Electronics and Avionics; Materials and Chemicals; Textiles and Other Manufacturers; and Metrology and Standards. The Boards provide assistance to suitable projects in industry or research organisations in the form of a grant or a shared cost contract.

Regional assistance

37. Regional development grant
Regional Development Grants are available in general to those who make capital investments for industrial development in the manufacturing sector in Special Development Areas and Development Areas.

38. Selective financial assistance
Financial assistance is available for investment projects creating or safeguarding employment in the assisted areas. It is essentially designed for firms in the manufacturing, mining and construction industries.

39. Office and service industries scheme
Grants are available to assist service industries to establish or expand in the Assisted Areas.

40. Contacts preference schemes
The Government gives preferential treatment to businesses in Special Development and Development Areas when tendering for contracts placed by Government Departments, nationalised industries and other public bodies.

41. European regional development fund
Assistance is available to develop new activities in steel and shipbuilding closure zones through the provision of consultancy information and services to small firms.

42. Enterprise zones
Eleven Enterprise Zones have been set up. Within these Zones both new and existing firms will benefit from certain tax concession, including exemptions from rates and Development Land Tax and 100% tax allowances for capital spending on industrial and commercial buildings. Planning procedures will be greatly simplified and remaining permissions speeded up. A further 12 zones are to be set up.

43. English industrial estates corporation (EIEC)
The Department of Industry provided £5m to the EIEC to enter into joint agreements with the private sector to construct small factories in the English Assisted Areas. So far agreements have been reached to the value of £30m to build over 1500 new small factory units.

Advisory services

44. Small firms service
The Department of Industry administers a Small Firms Service, which provides free information and advice on the wide range of problems encountered by those starting-up or running a small business.

45. Council for small industries in rural areas (COSIRA)
COSIRA provide consultancy, training courses and finance for small firms and retailers throughout rural areas.

46. Scottish Development Agency (SDA) and Highland and Islands Development Board (HIDB)
A wide range of advisory services are available from the SDA, including a general counselling service, training facilities and advice on marketing and exporting. General advice and finance are available to firms that approach the HIDB for financial help. In addition, 3 people have been appointed by the Board on a pilot scheme (50% EEC funded) to give specific advice to people setting up in business.

47. Welsh Development Agency and the Development Board for Rural Wales
The Welsh Development Agency (Small Business Unit) has 6 offices where Management Advisors can give general or specialist management advice. The Agency has Technical Advisors to give in-depth advice on

particular issues and financial help is also available. The Development Board for Rural Wales hold evening classes in 6 locations twice a year on 'Getting into Business'. The Board also organises in conjunction with the Manpower Services Commission a full-time 9 week Small Business Development Course. General business counselling and advice appointments can be arranged with the Board.

48. Local enterprise development unit
Gives business advice, in Northern Ireland, on subjects such as marketing, technology, accountancy and design. Finance is also available. The Unit's activities are mainly limited to firms employing up to 50 persons.

49. Enterprise agencies
The Department of the Environment and the Department of Industry are encouraging firms located in a particular area to pool their resources to help stimulate economic development by forming Local Enterprise Agencies. These are small bodies, usually staffed by secondees from the firms concerned, who provide help in a variety of ways, including the provision of advisory services, help with premises and matching potential investors with firms in need of capital. Much of this help is directed at stimulating small businesses. Tax relief has been made available to firms who contribute to approved agencies.

50. Tourist boards
The Welsh, English and Scottish Tourist Boards provide grants and advisory services.

Technical advice

51. Small firms technical enquiry service
Designed to help small firms with their technical problems and operated by the Production Engineering Research Association. This free service enables firms to have technical enquiries answered within an overall limit of 5 man-days of work.

52. Manufacturing Advisory Service (MAS)
Subsidised consultancy to factory units employing between 60 and 1000 people is available together with answers to technical questions involving manufacturing efficiency or competitiveness. MAS is operated by the Production Engineering Research Association.

53. Design Advisory Service
A free design advisory project involving up to 15 man-days work by a specialist consultant is available to production units with between 60 and 1000 employees. For a subsequent project the Design Advisory Service will meet half the cost. This scheme is operated by the Design Council.

54. Technology advisory point
A central contact point from which you can be directed to an appropriate source of expertise in a particular field (ie a departmental research establishment, research association or academic institution).

55. Microelectronics application project consultancy
Feasibility studies and consultancy support to encourage the application of microelectronics in all sectors of manufacturing industry.

56. Government laboratories
Department of Industry Laboratories have facilities which are unique in the country and they provide a wide range of technical services. They have national responsibilities in the field of measurement and standards; they provide calibration, analytical and other test services; and they undertake research into new techniques and materials of industrial importance. These Research and Development and technical services are an important feature of the Department's support for industry and are increasingly being used by companies on a repayment basis.

Employment

57. Unfair dismissal: the two year rule
The 1980 Employment Act gives a 2 year qualifying service period in respect of new employees for unfair dismissal complaints for firms with 20 or less workers.

58. Unfair dismissal: the size rule
This requires industrial tribunals to take account of the size and administrative resources of a firm in deciding on the fairness or unfairness of a dismissal.

59. Maternity provisions
The 1980 Employment Act relieves firms with 5 or fewer employees from the obligation to reinstate an employee after maternity leave where it is not reasonably practical to do so.
Relieve any employer of the obligation to reinstate after maternity leave if the employee declines an offer of suitable alternative work.

60. Enterprise allowance
A pilot experiment has been set up in five areas through the Small Firms Service and the Manpower Services Commission to give an Enterprise Allowance in the form of a grant for a period of one year to unemployed people who want to set up in business. The allowance will be available nationally from 1 August 1983.

Exports

61. British overseas trade board head office services
A wide range of export services and assistance from the BOTB to help at the various stages of the export process. The Board is a group of businessmen actively involved with exporting who guide and direct the Government's services and assistance to exporters.

62. Statistics and market intelligence library and the product data store
A range of published information on export markets is available from the Statistics and Market Intelligence Library and the Product Data Store both located in 1 Victoria Street, London, SW1. Telephone: 01-215 7877.

63. Market advisory service
The Market Advisory Service provides a modestly priced (currently £115) survey by the overseas Post of the potential of a product in a market and the key factors that will affect marketing. This will help the firm decide whether a visit would be worthwhile and, if the firm decides to proceed and the report supports it, the British Overseas Trade Board will contribute to the travel costs of an initial visit to the country.

64. Technical help for exporters
This is part of the British Standards Institution which for modest fees can help exporters to meet foreign standards and requirements and to anticipate the technical barriers to trade. The British Overseas Trade Board is sponsoring a free trial offer of up to £100 worth of technical advice for manufacturing firms with under 200 employees until the end of 1983.

65. Overseas status report service
A status report can be obtained through the Department of Trade to provide a check on the general standing (not financial reliability, which is done through a bank) of a possible agent or partner.

66. Export market research scheme
If professional detailed market research is needed, the BOTB's Export Market Research Scheme can provide a contribution towards the cost, and even towards the cost of consultancy to set up or reorganise a firm's export marketing department if necessary.

67. Missions and trade fairs
The British Overseas Trade Board offers attractive terms, through sponsoring organisations (mainly chambers of commerce and trade associations), for outward missions to visit overseas markets. Participation in an overseas trade fair on attractive terms is a feature of the joint venture scheme and can be either a way of testing a new market, or a direct-selling aid. There are special low rates for first — and second — time exhibitors.

68. Export intelligence service
The British Overseas Trade Board's Export Intelligence Service provides a computer — selected flow of opportunities for the product range and markets selected as soon as received from overseas posts and posted to subscribers daily as they arise for 35p a notice.

69. Market entry guarantee scheme
The risk of investment in the overhead costs of such facilities as offices, showrooms, warehouses, staff training etc where needed in the overseas market can be a serious deterrent to smaller firms, whereas they might be absorbed by a larger one. In recognition of this, the British Overseas Trade Board offers help with both finance and risk of this kind through the Market Entry Guarantee Scheme. The 50% financial contribution to these costs is paid back of the British Overseas Trade Board from a levy on sales in the market. No sales, no repayment — that is the guarantee part.

70. British overseas trade board: publicity unit
Firms may need help with publicity and promotion for exports at home and overseas. The Publicity Unit can give advice on the best methods and seek advice from overseas Posts. Help is given to exhibitors at trade fairs and to members of missions, and editorial coverage for novel products or success stories is secured wherever possible.
Recognising that smaller firms do not always have the same resources and hence the knowledge about government and other assistance, a special effort is made to publicise them. For example a recent series of conferences was aimed at bringing home to the new or small exporter the opportunities in Western Europe.

71. Simplification of international trade procedures board
There are many companies offering services to exporters to help with transport and clearance through customs and other procedures. The British Overseas Trade Board takes a particular interest in facilitating this aspect of trade through the Simplification of International Trade Procedures Board.

72. Exports credits guarantee department (ECGD)
ECGD provides insurance against default on payment by overseas buyers. Some of the major banks provide cover on a simpler basis under the umbrella of overall support from ECGD.

Planning relaxations

73. Light industrial/warehouse conversions
A planning application is no longer needed to change from light industrial to warehouse use or vice versa from premises of 235 square metres and below. Together with the existing provisions of the General Development Order this allows small firms to change their premises from general industrial to warehouse use without passing through the intermediate stage of light industrial use. However the reverse does not apply.

74. Extensions
No planning application is needed for extensions to industrial buildings of 20% subject to a maximum increase in floor area of 750 square metres. A planning application will be required, however, for any extension within 5 metres of the site boundary.

Training

75. Skill into business courses
Each course will cater for up to 20 people. The aim is to adapt and enhance existing skills (through a Skillcentre or college of further education) and to provide basic training through a college of further education in what it takes to plan, run and keep on top of a one-man business. The business training will centre on a training manual which will subsequently form the basis of an operating handbook. The course will provide free after-care through the Department of Industry's Small Firms Service.

76. New enterprise programme

77. Small business courses
The New enterprise programme is aimed at people who wish to launch businesses with major growth potential whilst the Small Business Courses are designed for people who plan to set up a more modest business venture. The courses are similar in format, with a residential period during which the trainees receive a grounding in the elements followed by a project period during which their learning is put into practice and their energies are directed towards getting their businesses off the ground.

78. The management extension programme
The programme operates under Training Opportunities Scheme and the Manpower Services Commission pays for the training of the redundant executives and pays them a weekly training allowance for the duration of their secondments. The participating firms are responsible only for meeting these secondees' out — of — pocket expenses.

79. In-plant training scheme
A grant is available to help with in-plant training costs associated with manufacturing projects which create jobs in Special Development Areas, Development Areas or, in exceptional circumstances, the Intermediate Areas.

Miscellaneous

80. Company law: reduced disclosure requirements
Under the Companies (Accounts) Regulations 1979 the particulars of turnover are from 1 January 1980 no longer required to be included where annual turnover is less than £1 million. The Companies Act 1981 further reduces the amount of detailed financial information that small companies must file with the Registrar of Companies. It also simplifies the arrangements for approval of company names.

81. Public purchasing: £5,000 rule
To facilitate small firms access to Government contracts, certain simplifications to the tendering and approval procedures are to be introduced.
Suppliers to most Government Departments will be exempt from normal approval procedures for contracts under £5,000.

82. Public purchasisng: non-approval rule
The government will allow non-approved firms to tender for non-urgent contracts and be subject to approval afterwards.

83. Energy survey scheme
Grants are provided to assist all sectors of the economy to employ consultants to carry-out energy-saving surveys.

84. Coal fired boiler scheme
A capital grant available to firms in the manufacturing industry are to agricultural and service concerns for the conversion or replacement of existing oil or gas firing equipment with coal firing.

85. Mineral exploration grants
A grant to offset costs incurred in exploring for, and evaluating for commercial purposes, mineral deposits in Great Britain.

86. Rates — right to pay by instalments
The Local Government Planning and Land Act introduced changes in the rating Laws which will benefit small businesses. One of these is the extension of the right to pay rates by instalments to those payable on business premises.

1983 Budget

The following announcements were made in March 1983.

87. Small engineering firms investment scheme
This scheme first ran between March and May 1982. It is being reintroduced from 28 March 1983. Grants will be available to help firms invest in certain types of advanced capital equipment. Almost all small and medium-sized engineering firms will qualify.

88. Marketing advisory service
The Department of Industry is currently considering a proposal from the Institute of Marketing to help establish a service to give advice on marketing to small and medium sized firms. In the meantime, advice on marketing can be obtained from the Small Firms Service.

Further information

For further information about any of these schemes telephone the operator (dial 100) and ask for Freefone 2444. You will be connected to the Small Firms Service. Ask for details of the appropriate scheme in which you are interested.
Some of the requirements are complex and you are best advised to seek advice initially from the Small Firms Service.

7. 12 Key Areas for Business Control

In different sections of this book I have mentioned some financial planning/business controls and other business techniques. In this short chapter, I have attempted to list by way of a summary, the factors I see as *Key Areas* for business control.

Check-list Key Areas	Actioned?
1. Business objectives.	
2. Management responsibilities and organisation.	
3. Product marketing/sales targets.	
4. Product production capacity.	
5. Product pricing.	
6. Stock control/purchases control.	
7. Creditor control.	
8. Debtor control.	
9. Overheads control/analysis.	
10. Capital expenditure budgeting.	
11. Financial performance monitoring **a** profit **b** cash flow	
12. Key performance indicators (ratios)	

Let us now look at each area in a little more detail.

Business objectives

— Have you developed clear objectives both short and long term?
— Are these objectives quantified in terms of market share; growth; product mix; rate of return?
— Have you built in review periods for your objectives and can you be flexible?
— Have you developed a financial plan and technical plan from these objectives?
— Are your objectives realistic?
— Don't forget high turnover is not necessarily the final answer; are you profitable?
— What is the significance of your objectives relative to your capital base?

Management responsibilities and organisation

— Are there gaps in key areas of management: general management; sales; production; finance and personnel?
— Do you have recruitment; training and promotion plans?
— Can your management team cope with expansion of the business?
— Do you have an organisational chart and is each job clearly defined?
— Have you delegated routine tasks as far as possible?
— Are management *accountable* for specific areas of responsibility?
— Are there clearly defined lines of reporting?
— Do you co-ordinate projects with a team responsibility?

Product marketing/sales targets

— What are the main factors affecting demand for your products? market competition; prices; quality; seasonability trends?
— Are your product lines expanding or declining?
— Do you plan and research for follow-on products?
— Do you have a well-spread customer base or are you in the hands of one or two main customers?
— Do you monitor sales goods returned as defective?
— Do you review 'make' or 'buy-in' decisions?
— Have you specific sales areas defined and sales targets set?

Product production capacity

— Do you plan production levels to link in with exports and sales?
— If sales are made from finished goods stock do you control lead-times correctly?
— Does your business have the physical production capability to meet planned sales?
— Do you have job cards setting out raw material requirements and estimating labour/machine hours for specific products?
— Do you plan for effective production runs rather than piece-work?
— Does your production controller liaise with your buyer to ensure an adequate, but not excessive, raw material stock?

Product Pricing

I know that it is difficult to set prices for new products, but pricing is a very important task

— Are costs estimated first to give a guideline to the price-setters?
— Are you careful in the giving of discounts for large orders or early payment?
— Are you careful to calculate the true 'cost' of discounts?
— Does your cost estimates include an element for future inflation?

— Do you price at the highest level acceptable in the market place?
— Do you endeavour to find out what your competitors are charging?
— What is the minimum price for your product to achieve break-even?
— Are there certain elements of product where you would be better off buying in rather than making?
— How frequently do you review prices?

Stock control/Purchases control

These two are closely related areas.
— What is the lead-time for your products?
— Are stocks kept to minimum acceptable levels for operational needs?
— **Pareto's** principle or the 80/20 rule can be useful in stock control i.e. does 20% of your stock articles represent 80% of the total stock value?
— Do you have a monthly review of stock holding?
— How often do you get quotes from new suppliers to check on purchasing prices?
— Can suppliers carry stock and make more frequent delivery to you?
— Are you careful not to buy in large quantities *just* to obtain a discount?
— Do you have separate stock level guides for raw materials/work-in-progress and finished goods?
— Do you dispose of obselete stock?
— Are you insured?

Creditor control

— Is your policy to take credit for as long as possible or do you pay quickly?
— Do you take discounts *when* appropriate?
— Do you review monthly creditors by age analysis? (see Chapter 2)
— Do you keep a close check on amounts owing to major suppliers?

Debtor control

— Do you nominate specific responsibility?
— Do you review monthly, using age-analysis? (see Chapter 2)
— Do you check on new customers for credit worthiness?
— What are your normal terms of trade?
— Are invoices despatched promptly?
— Do you send out statements regularly after the month-end?
— What is your bad-debt experience?
— Do you have a 'chase' letter system for outstanding debts?
— Do you take firm action against late payers?
— Can you get progress payments on large orders?

Overheads control/analysis

— Do you monitor monthly against budget?
— Do you closely monitor by analysis your major overhead items?
— Do you set overhead cost targets to individual departments where appropriate?
— Do you know minimum sales to cover annual overheads?

Capital expenditure budgeting

— Draw up annual budget and monitor monthly?
— Do you really need that expensive piece of plant?
— Is it for more than one particularly attractive order?
— Can payback of income etc. justify the outlay of cost?
— Consider leasing as an alternative?

Financial performance monitoring

a profit budget

— Is this monitored on a monthly/quarterly basis?
— Who is responsible for monitoring?
— Do you 'flex' the budget if circumstances change radically?
— Is the sales level being reached to cover break-even costs?
— Are you comparing results to last year's performance?

b cash budget

— Have you included *all* cash items?
— Are you monitoring monthly?
— Who is responsible?
— For format see Chapter 2.

(remember lack of cash can 'kill' your business)

Key performance indicators

— Break-even point being monitored?
— Ratios/percentages:

(i) $\frac{\text{Net Profit}}{\text{Total assets}} \times 100 = \ldots\%$

(ii) $\frac{\text{Sales}}{\text{Total assets}} =$

(iii) $\frac{\text{Profit}}{\text{Sales}} \times 100 = \ldots\%$

(iv) Gearing level $= \ldots :1$

I am sure that my list will not be exhaustive and there may well be other areas that you can think of.
However my list outlines the key points as I see them. I hope it's of use.

In Conclusion

I sincerely hope that this book has proved useful to you. Good luck and every success with your business.

Appendix

Bank of England

Banking Act 1979

List at 28 February 1982

1 Recognised banks

Alexanders Discount p.l.c.
Algemene Bank Nederland N.V.
Allied Arab Bank Ltd
Allied Bank International
Allied Bank of Pakistan Ltd
Allied Irish Banks Ltd
Allied Irish Investment Bank Ltd
American Express International Banking Corporation
American National Bank and Trust Company of Chicago
Amex Bank Ltd
Amsterdam-Rotterdam Bank N.V.
Anglo-Romanian Bank Ltd
Henry Ansbacher & Co. Ltd
A P Bank Ltd
Arab Bank Ltd
Arbuthnot Latham & Co. Ltd
Associated Japanese Bank (International) Ltd
Atlantic International Bank Ltd
Australia & New Zealand Banking Group Ltd

Banca Commerciale Italiana
Banca Nazionale del Lavoro
Banco Central, S.A.
Banco de Bilbao S.A.
Banco de la Nación Argentina
Banco de Santander, S.A.
Banco de Vizcaya S.A.
Banco di Roma S.p.A.
Banco do Brasil S.A.
Banco do Estado de Sao Paulo S.A.
Banco Espirito Santo e Comercial de Lisboa
Banco Exterior — U.K. S.A.
Banco Mercantil de Sao Paulo S.A.
Bancomer, S.A.
Banco Nacional de Mexico S.A.
Banco Real S.A.
Banco Totta & Acores E.P.
Banco Urquijo Hispano Americano Ltd
Bangkok Bank Ltd
Bank Brussels Lambert (U.K.) Ltd
Bank Bumiputra Malaysia Berhad
Bank für Gemeinwirtschaft A.G.
Bank Hapoalim B.M.
Bank Julius Baer & Co. Ltd
Bank Leumi (U.K.) Ltd
Bank Mellat
Bank Melli Iran
Bank of America International Ltd
Bank of America N.T. & S.A.
Bank of Baroda
The Bank of California N.A.
Bank of Ceylon
Bank of China
Bank of Cyprus (London) Ltd
Bank of India
The Bank of Ireland
Bank of London & South America Ltd
Bank of Montreal
Bank of New South Wales
The Bank of New York
Bank of New Zealand
The Bank of Nova Scotia
Bank of Scotland
The Bank of Tokyo, Ltd
Bank of Tokyo International Ltd
The Bank of Tokyo Trust Company
The Bank of Yokohama Ltd
Bank Saderat Iran
Bank Sepah
Bankers Trust Company
Banque Belge Ltd
Banque Belgo-Zairoise S.A.
Banque de L'Indochine et de Suez S.A.
Banque de Paris et des Pays-Bas S.A.
Banque Francaise de Credit International Ltd
Banque Francaise du Commerce Extérieur
Banque Nationale de Paris p.l.c.
Barclays Bank p.l.c.
Barclays Bank International Ltd
Barclays Merchant Bank Ltd
Baring Brothers & Co Ltd
Bayerische Hypotheken — und Wechsel — Bank A.G.
Bayerische Landesbank Girozentrale
Bayerische Vereinsbank
The British Bank of the Middle East
The British Linen Bank Ltd
Brown, Shipley & Co. Ltd

Canadian Imperial Bank of Commerce
Carolina Bank Ltd
Cater Allen p.l.c.
Centerre Bank N.A.
Central Bank of India

Central Trustee Savings Bank Ltd
The Chartered Bank
Charterhouse Japhet p.l.c.
Chase Bank (Ireland) Ltd
The Chase Manhattan Bank, N.A.
Chase Manhattan Ltd
Chemical Bank
Chemical Bank International Ltd
The Cho-Heung Bank, Ltd
Citibank N.A.
Citicorp International Bank Ltd
Clive Discount Company Ltd
Clydesdale Bank p.l.c.
The Commercial Bank of Australia Ltd
Commercial Bank of Korea Ltd
The Commercial Bank of the Near East Ltd
Commercial Bank of Wales p.l.c.
The Commercial Banking Company of Sydney, Ltd
Commerzbank A.G.
Commonwealth Trading Bank of Australia
Continental Illinois Ltd
Continental Illinois National Bank and Trust
Company of Chicago
Co-operative Bank p.l.c.
County Bank Ltd
Coutts & Co.
Crédit Industriel et Commercial
Crédit Lyonnais
Crédit Suisse
Credit Suisse First Boston Ltd
Creditanstalt — Bankverein
Credito Italiano
Crocker National Bank

The Dai-Ichi Kangyo Bank, Ltd
The Daiwa Bank, Ltd
The Detroit Bank & Trust Company
Deutsche Bank A.G.
Discount Bank (Overseas) Ltd
Dow Scandia Banking Corporation Ltd
Dresdner Bank A.G.

Euro-Latinamerican Bank Ltd
European Arab Bank Ltd
European Banking Company Ltd
European Brazilian Bank Ltd

The Fidelity Bank
First City National Bank of Houston
First Dallas Ltd
First Interstate Bank of California
First National Bank in Dallas
The First National Bank of Boston
The First National Bank of Chicago
First Pennsylvania Bank N.A.
First Wisconsin National Bank of Milwaukee
Robert Fleming & Co Ltd
French Bank of Southern Africa Ltd
The Fuji Bank, Ltd

Gerrard & National p.l.c.
Ghana Commercial Bank
Antony Gibbs & Sons, Ltd
Gillett Brothers Discount Company Ltd
Girard Bank
Gray Dawes Bank p.l.c.
Grindlay Brandts Ltd
Grindlays Bank p.l.c.
Guinness Mahon & Co. Ltd
Gulf International Bank B.S.C.

Habib Bank A.G. Zurich
Habib Bank Ltd
Hambros Bank Ltd
Hanil Bank
Harris Trust and Savings Bank
Havana International Bank Ltd
Hessische Landesbank — Girozentrale —
Hill Samuel & Co. Ltd
C. Hoare & Co.
The Hokkaido Takushoku Bank, Ltd
The Hongkong and Shanghai Banking Corporation
Hungarian International Bank Ltd

The Industrial Bank of Japan, Ltd
International Commercial Bank p.l.c.
International Energy Bank Ltd
International Mexican Bank Ltd
International Westminster Bank p.l.c.
Irving Trust Company
Italian International Bank Ltd

Japan International Bank Ltd
Jessel, Toynbee p.l.c.
Johnson Matthey Bankers Ltd
Leopold Joseph & Sons Ltd

King & Shaxson p.l.c.
Kleinwort, Benson Ltd
Korea Exchange Bank
Korea First Bank
The Kyowa Bank, Ltd

Lazard Brothers & Co., Ltd
Libra Bank Ltd
Lloyds Bank p.l.c.
Lloyds Bank International Ltd
Lloyds Bank International (France) Ltd
London & Continental Bankers Ltd
London Interstate Bank Ltd
The Long-Term Credit Bank of Japan, Ltd

Malayan Banking Berhad
Manufacturers Hanover Ltd
Manufacturers Hanover Trust Company
Marine Midland Bank N.A.
Mellon Bank, N.A.
Mercantile Bank Ltd
Merrill Lynch International Bank Ltd
Midland Bank p.l.c.
Midland and International Banks p.l.c.
The Mitsubishi Bank Ltd
The Mitsubishi Trust and Banking Corporation
The Mitsui Bank Ltd
The Mitsui Trust & Banking Company Ltd

Samuel Montagu & Co. Ltd
Morgan Grenfell & Co. Ltd
Morgan Guaranty Trust Company of New York
Moscow Narodny Bank Ltd
Muslim Commercial Bank Ltd

National Bank of Abu Dhabi
The National Bank of Australasia Ltd
National Bank of Canada
National Bank of Detroit
National Bank of Greece S.A.
The National Bank of New Zealand Ltd
National Bank of Pakistan
National Westminster Bank p.l.c.
Nedbank Ltd
The Nippon Credit Bank, Ltd
Noble Grossart Ltd
Nordic Bank p.l.c.
North Carolina National Bank
Northern Bank Ltd
The Northern Trust Company

Orion Royal Bank Ltd
Oversea-Chinese Banking Corporation Ltd
Overseas Union Bank Ltd

Page & Gwyther Ltd
Philippine National Bank
Privatbanken Ltd
Punjab National Bank

Qatar National Bank S.A.Q.
Gerald Quin, Cope & Co. Ltd

Rafidain Bank
Rea Brothers Ltd
P.S. Refson & Co. Ltd
Republic Bank Dallas, N.A.
Reserve Bank of Australia
The Riggs National Bank of Washington, D.C.
N. M. Rothschild & Sons Ltd
The Royal Bank of Canada
The Royal Bank of Canada (London) Ltd
The Royal Bank of Scotland Ltd
The Royal Trust Company of Canada

The Saitama Bank Ltd
The Sanwa Bank, Ltd
Saudi International Bank
(Al-Bank Al-Saud Al-Alami Ltd)
Scandinavian Bank Ltd
J. Henry Schroder Wagg & Co. Ltd
Seattle — First National Bank
Seacombe Marshall & Campion p.l.c.
Security Pacific National Bank
Singer & Friedlander Ltd
Smith St. Aubyn & Co. Ltd
Société de Banque Occidentale pour l'industrie et le commerce
Société Générale Bank Ltd
Société Générale pour favoriser le développement du commerce et de l-industrie en France
Sonali Bank

The Standard Bank p.l.c.
Standard Chartered Bank p.l.c.
Standard Chartered Merchant Bank Ltd
State Bank of India
The Sumitomo Bank, Ltd
The Sumitomo Trust and Banking Company Ltd
Swiss Bank Corporation
Syndicate Bank

The Taiyo Kobe Bank Ltd
Texas Commerce Bank N.A.
The Thai Farmers Bank Ltd
The Tokai Bank, Ltd
The Toronto-Dominion Bank
Toronto Dominion International Bank Ltd
The Tokyo Trust & Banking Company Ltd
Teade Development Bank

UBAF Bank Ltd
Ulster Bank Ltd
Union Bank of Switzerland
The Union Discount Company of London Ltd
United Bank Ltd
The United Bank of Kuwait Ltd
United Commercial Bank
United Overseas Bank Ltd

S. G. Warburg & Co. Ltd
Wells Fargo Bank N.A.
Westdeutsche Landesbank Girozentrale
Williams & Glyn's Bank Ltd
Wintrust Securities Ltd
Württembergische Kommunale Landesbank Girozentrale

The Yasuda Trust and Banking Co., Ltd
Yorkshire Bank p.l.c.

Zambia National Corporation

2 Licensed deposit-taking institutions

A1 (Investment) Ltd
Abbey Finance Co. Ltd
Afghan National Credit & Finance Ltd
African Continental Bank Ltd
The Alliance Trust p.l.c.
Allied Irish Finance Co. Ltd
Al Saudi Banque S.A.
Altajir Ltd
Anglo-Yugoslav (LDT) Ltd
Arab Bank Investment Co. Ltd
Arab Banking Corporation B.S.C.
Armada Investments Ltd
Assemblies of God Property Trust
Associated Credits Ltd
Associates Capital Corporation Ltd
Auban Finance Ltd
Avco Trust Ltd

Banca Serfin, S.A.
Banco de Jerez S.A.
Banco di Sicilia

Banco Português do Atlántico
Bank America Finance Ltd
Bank Handlowy w Warszawie S.A.
Bank of Credit and Commerce International S.A.
Bank of Ireland Finance Ltd
Bank of Ireland Finance (N.I.) Ltd
The Bank of Nova Scotia Trust Company (United Kingdom) Ltd
Bank of Oman Ltd
Bank Street Securities Ltd
Bank Tejarat
Bankers Trust International Ltd
Banque du Rhone et de la Tamise S.A.
The Baptist Union Corporation Ltd
Barbados National Bank
Barclays Bank Trust Company Ltd
Barclays Bank UK Ltd
Thomas Barlow & Bro. Ltd
B.C.F. Finance Co. Ltd
Beaver Investments Ltd
Beirut Rivad Bank S.A.L.
Beneficial Trust Ltd
Berliner Bank A.G.
Boston Trust & Savings Ltd
Bowmaker Ltd
Bradford Investments
Bremar Holdings Ltd
Bridgeover Ltd
Bridgeway Finance Ltd
Bristol & West Investments Ltd
British Credit Trust Ltd
Brook Securities & Co. Ltd
Brutton Mortgage Investments (Hampshire) Ltd
Buchanan Securities Ltd
Bucks Land & Building Co. Ltd
Bunge & Co. Ltd
Burlington Investments Ltd
Business Mortgages & Investment Trust p.l.c.
Bablos Bank S.A.L.

Calculus Finance Ltd
Canada Permanent Trust Co. (U.K.) Ltd
Cassa di Risparmio delle Provincie Lombarde
Castle Court Trust Ltd
Castle Phillips Finance Co. Ltd
Cattles Holdings Finance Ltd
Cavendish Guaranty Trust Ltd
Cayzer Ltd
Cedar Holdings Ltd
Century Factors Ltd
Century Industrial Services Ltd
Chancellor Finance Ltd
Chancery Securities Ltd
Charter Consolidated Financial Services Ltd
Chartered Trust p.l.c.
Charterhouse Japhet Credit Ltd
Chesterfield Street Trust Ltd
CP Choularton, Sons & Partners Ltd
The Chuo Trust & Banking Company Ltd
Citibank Trust Ltd
City Trust Ltd
Close Brothers Ltd
Clydesdale Bank Finance Corporation Ltd
CE Coates & Co. Ltd
Cobnar Finance Co. Ltd
Colonial Bank
Combined Capital Ltd
Commercial Credit Services Ltd
Commonwealth Savings Bank of Australia
Consolidated Credits & Discounts Ltd
Co-operative Bank (Commercial) Ltd
Corinthian Securities Ltd
Coutts Finance Co.
Craneheath Securities Ltd
Crédit du Nord
Cross & Bevingtons (Finance) Ltd
Cue & Co.
Cyprus Credit Bank Ltd
Cyprus Finance Corporation (London) Ltd
The Cyprus Popular Bank

Dalbeattie Finance Co. Ltd
Darlington Merchant Credits Ltd
Darlington & Co. Ltd
Dawnay, Day & Co. Ltd
Deutsche Genossenschaftsbank
The Development Bank of Sinagpore Ltd
Dunbar & Co. Ltd
Duncan Lawrie Ltd
Dunsterville Allen Ltd

Eagil Trust Co. Ltd
East Anglian Securities Trust Ltd
East Midlands Finance Co. Ltd
Eastcheap Investments Ltd
Eccles & District Finance Co. Ltd
The English Association Trust Ltd
Ensign Discount Co. Ltd
Equatorial Trust Corporation Ltd
E. T. Trust Ltd
Everett Chettle Associates
Exeter Trust Ltd

Family Finance Ltd
F. & C. Management Ltd
Farmers (WCF) Finance Ltd
Federated Trust Corporation Ltd
FFI (UK Finance) p.l.c.
FIBI Financial Trust Ltd
Finance for Industry p.l.c.
Financial and General Securities Ltd
James Finlay Corporation Ltd
Finova Finance Ltd
First Co-operative Fiance Ltd
First Guarantee Trust Co. Ltd
First Indemnity Credit Ltd
First Knightsbridge Guarantee Ltd
First National Bank of Maryland
First National Bank of Minneapolis
First National Boston Ltd
First National Securities Ltd
Ford Financial Trust Ltd
Ford Motor Credit Co. Ltd
Forward Trust Ltd
Robert Fraser & Partners Ltd

Gavel Finance
Gillespie Bros. & Company Ltd
Girozentrale und Bank der österreichischen Sparkassen A.G.
Goode Durrant Trust Ltd
Goodwin Squires Securities Ltd
H.T. Greenwood Ltd
Gereetwell Finance Ltd
Gresham Trust Ltd
Greyhound Guaranty Ltd
Grindlays Bank (Scotland) Ltd
Grindlays Humberclyde Ltd
G.T. Management Ltd

The Hardware Federation Finance Co. Ltd
Hargrave Securities Ltd
Harrods Trust Ltd
Harton Securities Ltd
Harwal Finance Group Ltd
The Heritable & General Trust Ltd
H.F.C. Trust Ltd
H. & J. Finance Co. (Midlands) Ltd
Hobart Securities Ltd
Holdenhurst Securities Ltd
Houston Financial Services Ltd
Hume Corporation Ltd

IBJ International Ltd
Industrial Funding Trust Ltd
Industrial National Bank of Rhode Island
The Investment Bank of Ireland Ltd
Investment Trustees Ltd
Iran Overseas Investment Corporation Ltd

Jabac Finances Ltd
Joliman Finance Ltd

Keesler Federal Credit Union
Kintyre Securities Ltd
Knowsley & Co. Ltd

Lloyds & Scottish Ltd
Lloyds & Scottish Trust Ltd
Lloyds Bank (LABCO) Ltd
Lodhi Finance Ltd
Lombard & Ulster Ltd
Lombard North Central Ltd
Lombard Street Investment Trust Co. Ltd
London Law Securities Ltd
London Scottish Finance Corporation p.l.c.
Lordsvale Finance Ltd

McNeill Pearson Ltd
Mallinhall Ltd
Manchester Exchange Trust Ltd
W.M. Mann & Co. (Investments) Ltd
Edward Manson & Co. Ltd
Manufacturers Hanover Export Finance Ltd
Manufacturers Hanover Industrial Finance Ltd
The Mardun Investment Co. Ltd
Matheson Trust Co. Ltd
Medens Trust Ltd
Meghrai & Sons Ltd

Mercantile Credit Company Ltd
Merchant Banking (N.I.) Ltd
Mercury Provident Society Ltd
Merseyside Finance Ltd
The Methodist Chapel Aid Association Ltd
M.H. Credit Corporation Ltd
MMH Investments Ltd
Middle East Bank Ltd
Midland Bank Finance Corporation Ltd
Midland Bank Industrial Equity Holdings Ltd
Midland Bank Trust Company Ltd
Milford Mutual Facilities Ltd
Minster Trust Ltd
Moneycare Ltd
Moorgate Mercantile Holdings p.l.c.
Mortgage Management & Investments Ltd
Multibanco Comermex S.A.
Musket Finance Ltd
Mynshul Trust Ltd

National Bank of Fort Sam Houston
National Bank of Nigeria Ltd
National Commercial & Glyns Ltd
National Guardian Finance Corporation Ltd
Nederlandsche Middenstandsbnk N.V.
New Nigeria Bank Ltd
M.J.H. Nightingale & Co. Ltd
N.I.I.B. Group Ltd
North West Securities Ltd
The North of Scotland Finance Co. Ltd
Northern Bank Development Corporation Ltd
Northern Bank Executor & Trustee Company Ltd
Northern Ireland Industrial Bank (I.O.M.) Ltd
Norwich General Trust Ltd
Nowet (Financiers) Ltd

Oriental Credit Ltd
Overseas Trust Bank Ltd
Park Street Securities Ltd
The People's Trust & Savings Ltd
Personal Loans (Investments) Ltd
Phibrobank A.G.
PKB Investments Ltd
Pointon York Ltd
Prestwick Investment Trust Ltd
PSP & Company (U.K.) Ltd
Punjab & Sind Bank

R. Raphael & Sons Ltd
Rathbone Bros. & Co.
Reliance Trust Ltd
Republic National Bank of New York
Rhone Trust Ltd
Roxburghe Guarantee Corporation Ltd

St. Margaret's Trust Ltd
St. Martin-le-Grand Securities Ltd
David Sassoon & Co. Ltd
Saturn Investment Management Co. Ltd
Savings Bank of South Australia
Schroder Leasing Ltd
E.S. Schwab & Co. Ltd
Shanghai Commercial Bank Ltd

Shawlands Securities Ltd
The Siam Commercial Bank, Ltd
N.V. Slavenburg's Bank
Smith & Williamson Securities
South Notts Finance Ltd
Southsea Mortgage & Investment Co. Ltd
S. P. Finance Ltd
Spring Gardens Securities p.l.c.
Spry Finance Ltd
Standard Credit Services Ltd
Standard Property Investment Co. Ltd
State Bank of Victoria
Sterling Credit Ltd
Swiss Bank Corporation International Ltd

TCB Ltd
The Teachers & General Investment Co. Ltd
Texas Commerce International Ltd
Thorncliffe Finance Ltd
Treesford Securities Ltd
Treloan Ltd
Tricity Acceptance Ltd
Trinity Trust & Savings Ltd
Trucanda Trusts Ltd
Turkish Bank Ltd
Tyndall & Co.

Ulster Bank Trust Company
Ulster Investment Bank Ltd
Unico Finance Ltd
Union Bank of India
United Dominions Trust Ltd
Universal Credit Ltd

Barrie Vanger & Co. Ltd
Venture Finance Ltd
Vernons Trust Corporation

Wagon Finance Ltd
Wallace, Smith Trust Co. Ltd
Wells Fargo Ltd
West Riding Securities Ltd
Western Trust & Savings Ltd
Whiteaway Laidlaw & Co. Ltd
Wimbledon & South West Finance Co. Ltd
N. H. Woolley & Co. Ltd

Yorkshire Bank Finance Ltd
Yorkshire Bank Leasing Ltd
H. F. Young & Co. Ltd

NOTES

NOTES

NOTES

NOTES

NOTES

NOTES

NOTES

NOTES

NOTES

NOTES